The 1889 Camp Meeting Sermons

Sermons by
Alonzo T. Jones, Ellen G. White
and others

TEACH Services, Inc.
P U B L I S H I N G
www.TEACHServices.com • (800) 367-1844

Copyright © 1998, 2013 TEACH Services, Inc.
ISBN-13: 978-1-4796-0210-0 (Paperback)
ISBN-13: 978-1-57258-860-8 (ePub)
ISBN-13: 978-1-57258-861-5 (Kindle)
Library of Congress Control Number: 2013941439

Published by

TEACH Services, Inc.
P U B L I S H I N G
www.TEACHServices.com • (800) 367-1844

Schedule of Sermons

THE CAMP MEETING

The Adventists Celebrate The Seventh Day At Ottawa

As One of Rest and Protest Against Religious Legislation—
Elder Jones' Description of "Constitutional Rights"
—Interesting Discourses.

Special Correspondence of the CAPITAL

FOREST PARK, OTTAWA, KAN., MAY 5...

THE DAY OPENED AT THE CAMP MEETING ON SATURDAY all that could be desired and continued so. Early at 5 o'clock the campers began to rise and in half an hour were assembled for the morning worship in the tabernacle. At 9 o'clock came the Sabbath school; at half past 10, the morning sermon; at half past 2, the afternoon discourse; at sundown, the evening Sabbath worship, and at 8, the lecture. Visitors were numerous at all the day convocations, and at night the assembly hall was filled to its utmost seating capacity, many standing.

The number of classes formed in the Sabbath school was twenty-eight, five of them in the primary divisions, with a total membership of 228, of which twenty-seven were children. The lesson in the senior division was: "Unsanctified Service and the Result." In the primary, "The Life of Christ." Elder E.H. Gates reviewed the senior division, and Elder W.W. Hyatt the primary. The first named is from the Colorado Conference and the latter from Nebraska.

The following is a summary of the last quarterly report (just prepared) of the Seventh-day Adventist Sabbath schools of Kansas: number of schools reporting, 75; membership, 2,139; average attendance, 1,607; donations, $123.25.

The morning sermon, at 10:30 on Sabbath, was delivered by Elder A.T. Jones.

ELDER JONES' SERMON

THE SPEAKER TOOK HIS TEXT FROM EXODUS 20:8—"Remember the Sabbath day to keep it holy." "This," he said, "is practically the fourth commandment, telling us what it is, and what we are to do with it, the balance being simply explanatory. The latter part of the commandment gives the reasons why we should observe it—we are to rest because God rested, and to keep it holy because He did. Again, it is, 'Remember the Sabbath day to keep it holy,' not 'and keep it holy,' as is often quoted. If we do not remember to keep it holy we cannot keep it holy when it comes to us. This is why the word 'to' is placed there, the definition of the word being in substance a motion toward an object. Now, then, where does our observance of this Sabbath begin? When did Adam's observance begin? Why, just when the first Sabbath was past, because Adam did not keep the first one, as God had to rest before a Sabbath was fully born, so that as soon as the sun went down on the first Sabbath Adam began to 'remember to' keep the coming Sabbath; so should we do likewise. We therefore are to keep the commandment all the week up to Friday, and then begin to keep the Sabbath also, so that on the Sabbath we keep both the commandment and the Sabbath. It is plain then that all we do during the week should be done in reference to the coming Sabbath. If we fail to do this we are often placed in perplexing positions by having goods delivered, or business, or work overlooked pressed upon us on the Sabbath. If, then, we think to keep the commandment, we can keep the Sabbath when it comes, but otherwise we cannot. The keeping of the Sabbath holy, begins at once when the Sabbath comes. We cannot carry our work right up to the hour of its beginning or get so behind with our work that we have to crowd Friday full of work and overstep the time into the Sabbath to close up, and then keep the day holy. We have already profaned holy time and we cannot then comply with God's requirements.

"Now let us notice another point. The commandment is not given, as men assert, because of man's physical necessities. Man's physical nature or needs are not considered at all. Man's spiritual nature alone is considered. Man is to rest simply because God did so. Not because his physical nature needs it. Now, if a man works so hard that on the Sabbath he has to rest to refresh his body, that to violate the Sabbath instead of keeping it holy. If we come up to the Sabbath capable of talk delight in it, then we are blessed and able to keep it holy. This argument that man needs a day of rest in seven is a fraud and based upon a fraud. There is nothing in the commandment or its requirements in reference to man's physical wants. But suppose we come up to the Sabbath in a proper way, how are we to keep it when it comes? In Leviticus 23:3 it is ordered that there shall be a holy convocation on that day–an assembly of the people, so that one of the duties is to have a meeting for God's praise and worship. Now I want to show that it is our spiritual needs and not our physical needs considered. God did not rest because He was weary, hence His physical needs were not considered; neither are ours, as we rest because He did. Isaiah tells us so in chapter 40:28. Nothing, then, which He gives can lessen what He has to give. Exodus 31:16,17 tells us why we should rest. The idea of God being 'refreshed' is, in the Hebrew, that 'He took delight in the creation He had formed,' and this is certainly the only view of rest we can conceive of God. He being a spirit, it could only be a spiritual rest, and we rest because He did, then our rest must be a spiritual one, and the refreshing a spiritual refreshing." The speaker then read from the first chapters of Genesis to show how God saw all He had created as very good and delighted in it.

"Now then let us read why the Sabbath was given by reading Psalm 111:4. It is a sign by which we are ever to remember the Creator and why we keep His Sabbath. Now, then, how shall we keep it? Let us read Psalm 92:1,4 especially the last. God delighted in His work, and David says we are to be glad for the same reason, and we are to delight in it, that it lifts us up to God and makes us know more of Him, His goodness and power. I am perfectly satisfied that God blessed the seventh day, and that there is a blessing that goes with it that no other day has, and when we realize our duty to remember to keep it, we will feel this sacredness more than we do now. We may hear preaching all the week, but when we listen to it on Sabbath it seems more sacred and consecrated. Well, then, if on the Sabbaths we lift our hearts to God we will feel nearer to Him, and if we contemplate His works to delight in them, we shall be blessed. I believe it to be part of the commandment to take our children out in the fields on the Sabbath day and point out the beauties of creation leading their minds up to God. If we act in this way we are keeping the Sabbath as God did, delighting in it, and our children will look forward to it also with delight, instead of fancying it to be a burden."

The speaker then narrated an anecdote of Kepler, the astronomer, when he discovered the real motion and orbits of the planets, and exclaimed, "I think the thoughts after Thee, O God!"

"Now that is what David says in the Psalms; brethren let us try to think God's thoughts after Him, and so daily discover new beauties and grandeur in God's creation, and our minds will be elevated to Him, will be filled with love and gratitude to God who enables us to understand His goodness toward us, and we will delight in His appointed day on which we can draw nearer to Him and be refreshed. We can all be Keplers, in our own sphere, so, brethren, let us do it."

He then gave a number of illustrations to show the magnitude of the power of God (describing the Gulf Stream; the different texture in woody fiber growing in cold and warm climates; and showing how the snowdrop is, by the law of gravitation, compelled to droop its head to become fruitful, and that to accomplish it God must have weighed the earth, to regulate the gravitation, or else the first snow-drop would have been the last), to prove to his hearers that God wanted man to investigate such things, and to understand them, that they may know Him better and delight in His creative power. "These are all for our contemplation and delight on the Sabbath day. And this is not all. We have eternal salvation to study and contemplate and delight in. In Ephesians 3:8,11, the last particularly, shows that in the Gospel of Jesus Christ, the Lord is trying to make man understand something about His eternal purposes. Read Ephesians 2:4–6, which tells us it will be our study in the age to come. This life is merely the beginning of our study of God, His creation and His purposes in reference to Him. It will be the science and song of eternity. The Lord has given us the Sabbath for the purpose of thinking His thoughts after Him, delighting in His creative power, and drawing nearer to Him and to find the joy of the Lord in Him and to rejoice in Him because we know Him as He is."

AFTERNOON SERVICES...

There was quite a turnout of citizens at the afternoon services and extra chairs had to be provided. The interest to hear among the residents of Ottawa seems to be increasing, and as the weather is growing more favorable, it is hoped that the large tabernacle can soon be used. The Electric Light company has been busy at work putting in lights in this building and the park, and very shortly all portions will have the benefit of this light. The afternoon sermon in the assembly room was delivered by Elder E.H. Gates of Colorado. The speaker said:

SERMON BY ELDER GATES

"I WILL CALL YOUR ATTENTION TO I JOHN 3:1–3. The apostle begins by calling our attention to the wonderful love of God. It seems that he can not, and no one can, describe it. He says: 'Behold!' It will hurt no one, brethren, to call our attention to God's love and what He has done for us. When I first embraced the truth I could see well enough His justice in calling us to account for our sins, but I believe there is another side to His character. At first I looked upon God as one who was to be dreaded, and looking for failures in His people. I do not entertain that idea now. I was brought up to believe in an endless pit of torment, but at the age of 20 years I learned the true character of God, and I can not express the feeling that came over me at the discovery. It came from reading a little work carefully, depicting the popular view of Satan as a hideous monster, and I read the writer's ridicules of this idea. I hardly dared believe it was all false, but I thought if this writer can prove it out of the Bible he has a right to do so, and further, I have a right to trace it out too. I read the book through and by that time my ideas had changed–I knew then that God was not a tyrant ready to destroy His people but a God of tender mercy and love, yet it took time to fully eradicate my old notions. For the last year I have been studying more closely the character of God, as one desirous of making us sons of His. We are liable to look upon God in a different light to what He is, because, as Mrs. White says, Satan has mislead the world and taught them to misunderstand God and His relations toward them."

The Elder then narrated an anecdote of a minister attending a dying sinner and for three visits only held up God's justice, until the man cried out, "Is there no help out of this?" And this gave him the opportunity and the visitor opened the Bible, and taught him of the matchless love of Christ, and the man repented and was converted. Now, as men have been so deceived how can they learn the true character of God? Why, by this wording, as this minister did the word of God. He read John 14:7–9. This says that those who saw Christ saw the Father, they being identical. What was Christ? A loving, tender Lord, going about doing good, healing the sick and forgiving the sinner. Everywhere He went He dispensed blessings. God is love, brethren, and now He has adopted His people and made them sons and daughters; Paul says so in Romans 8:14–16. It is this adoption that enables us to cry Abba, Father! God takes those who come to Him and makes them sons. John tells us to such He gives the right or privilege of becoming sons and daughters. How honored we would feel to be admitted to some foreign court; even to be admitted to a sight of the president of the United States, or receive a shake of his hand, we would feel highly honored.

"But suppose we could be adopted into some royal family, it would be looked upon as a great honor, because it would carry with it a privilege of becoming heirs. Dear brethren, we have not been adopted into an earthly family, but a heavenly–adoption into the Royal Family of God. John says that 'the Spirit beareth witness with our spirit that we are sons of God, and if sons, heirs,' that is, we are adopted, and thus take His name, and become heirs. Remember the promise to Abraham; all the world was to be his, and his seed. Who is the seed? Let us read Galatians 3 and we find it is Christ. The promise is to Abraham and Christ then, and verse 29 shows us how we become heirs according to this promise, and my text shows the love that has been shown us, that we are to be adopted into His family and become His children. The longer I live I want to study this side of God's character, and to realize His love and goodness toward us. I fear we are not enjoying our religion as we should, but maybe we have been making the same mistake that the Jews did, stumbling at the stumbling stone (spoken of by St. Paul in Romans 9) which is Christ. We have sometimes felt as the fanatics who mutilate their bodies by the way of penance to get a little better before coming to Christ, in reality doing as the Jews did of old, 'going about to establish our own righteousness.' I am so thankful today, brethren, that we know of the love of God, and that God is willing to forgive and accept us and own us as His sons and daughters, and I feel that it will do no harm to tell others about it."

9

After giving many beautiful illustrations showing the tender love and pitying watch care exercised over the union, by the Lord who does not take delight in the death of any soul, he closed by calling attention to the fact that the only reminder there will be in the new earth of sin and the curse of this will be the marks of the nails of the cross in the palms of our Lord's hands, and earnestly pleading with all to believe in the tender love of the One who has graven their names in the palms of His hands.

At the close of the discourse the order of exercise was changed and the meeting turned into an "experience meeting," in which a large number of short and tender testimonies were given. This portion of the exercises seemed to be of especial interest to the visitors present. After an hour spent in this way the congregation separated to come together again a half hour before sunset (the close of the Sabbath) to seek God in prayer, after which Elder Jones began the delivery of the evening lecture on the—

"EVILS OF RELIGIOUS LEGISLATION"

THE SPEAKER SAID: "IN BEGINNING THE STUDY of civil government and religion we will take the Declaration of Independence to start with. All men are born free and equal, and endowed with certain inalienable rights. At that time this was a new statement, because there had been monarchical forms of government for ages, men being born noble, so-called, and recognized as such, but our country denied the nobility of birth and asserted all men to be free and equal in matters of rights, and so every man in this nation has all the rights of all others, and with a right to assert them. The president has no other right than the humblest citizen. He has more authority but no additional rights. Senators and other law makers are servants, we, the people, the masters. The president has only delegated authority, receiving it from the people, so that in this country there are no rulers except the people. Every man, then, is a master and a ruler, and those we elect are our servants, serving more or less according to their office. This is not a new idea, but the very one our fathers had in view when they made the Declaration. President Lincoln declared our government to be a government 'of the people, by the people, and for the people.' If all would abide by this declaration we would indeed be a happy people. The Declaration of Independence embodies the very ideas expressed in Christ's gospel, that of perfect liberty. When a republic reaches that point where they cease to govern themselves, a power will arise to govern them, so that the republic will cease to exist, even ours. As we are then equal, with equal rights, how does a government arise? Each has the right to assert his right; but for the good of all, each surrenders certain rights, but there are some that are inalienable rights and cannot be delegated, among them being life, liberty and the pursuit of happiness. There are others which we will notice presently. If each retain all his rights and asserted them independently, no one would be as well off as he would by surrendering certain ones; therefore each one does so surrender some for the good of all. For instance, each one has the right of self protection of person, family, and property; but as all do not recognize the right, some invade the rights of others, so the amount of single protection one possesses is not adequate. Hence men combine for the purpose of obtaining the benefit of the combined strength of all, so that each receives in turn a thousand fold what he so surrenders. It is the interest therefore of all men to enter into some such compact, and the result is civil government, so that statement is true, and asserts that governments derive their powers from the governed."

The speaker then read from the Massachusetts Bill of Rights to substantiate his statements. "Commonwealth," he said, "means common wealth–common good and that is what governments are organized for. But there are certain rights that no man can surrender and be a man, and one of these is the right of conscience. The commonwealth of Massachusetts (as an example) admits this, and says that no man can ever receive an equivalent for them. No man can surrender, for instance, his right to believe, at least no man has any right to do so—the right to search the Scriptures for himself, find out the truth for himself, and obey it for himself—to any man or any form of government. Now we come to consider the denial of the right of any government to legislate in matters of religion. It has no right to legislate against or in favor of, what any man believes. It has no right to legislate in favor of or against Christianity. Men can never assent to legislation in favor of the religion they profess without surrendering their right of belief, because they surrender their right to change their belief afterward, so that, in doing so, men surrender their religious liberty.

"Ever deny then the power of government to legislate in favor of what you believe. This is genuine assertion of religious liberty. Tell this to others also, because the assertion of religious liberty has not reached this point. The assertion of my right to believe as I please is not true religious liberty, but my assertion of your right to believe as you please is true religious liberty."

The speaker then quoted Macaulay's ironical argument that the majority have the right to assert their belief and force the minority to change their belief to harmonize with their own. "The time has come, however, for us to assert the right of others to believe as they please, and to assert it at all times and places. If you or I sit idly down and see another's rights invaded and taken away, and do nothing, because it does not harm us we will have no right to complain when ours are invaded. The true solution, then, of the problem is to assert the rights of others. The question is not who is right, but what are the individual rights. The Baptist has the right to believe as he does but he has no right to compel the Methodist to act as if he was a Baptist, and so of all denominations, every man having a right to be what he pleases, but not the right to use the civil power to compel any man to respect any religion. A man has a right to be an infidel or Christian as he pleases and no one has the right to interfere with him. So long as the Constitution stands as it is, all are protected in their rights and even though infidels or Catholics filled all the seats in Congress they could pass no laws hurtful to Christianity, because the Constitution forbids religious legislation. Now, brethren, in announcing our position, bear in mind that we stand on the Constitution and Declaration of Independence."

THE INSTITUTE

AT 9:15 EACH MORNING THE INSTITUTE COMES TOGETHER for the purpose of asking questions on previous lectures and sermons in order to give opportunity for elucidation of points not made clear or not sufficiently elaborated. The Institute class of 100 members took up to begin with, Elder A.T. Jones' opening lecture on the "Evils of Religious Legislation." In reply to inquiries from the elder it was found that, although our government is founded on the Declaration of Independence, scarcely any of the class had ever read it through. In reply to a question as to what the Declaration declares, the reply was "all men are born free and equal," but it does not say so, the words being, "all men are created equal." The elder took this mode of showing all the necessity of quoting an authority correctly. Alienable rights were defined as follows: An alien is a foreigner. To be alienable is to be able to give up rights, and not be able to assert rights. An Englishman alienates himself in leaving England and is an alien in America, giving up the rights he had in England and unable to assert his English rights in America. Inalienable rights, therefore, are the opposite of alienate, that is, they can not be abrogated or given away, such as life, liberty and the pursuit of happiness. Life can only be alienated by suicide, not his liberty, or those things that pertain to the proper enjoyment of life. All just powers are derived from the consent of the governed. They derive only just powers, unjust powers derived is usurpation, tyranny and despotism. When the people are all equal, all the people have the rights and consent of all that gives the power to government. The first thing a band of men coming together have to do is to organize, and that is government. Therefore government is inherent in the very nature of things among men. The principle of inherent right is that of religious liberty. If men had considered life the dearest, very little progress would have ever been made in Christianity. The Declaration of Independence mentions these inalienable rights but religious liberty is dearer and more important than all these. Some men have loved their civil liberties better than their life, and because of this the world eventually emerges from despotism.

The morning hour was occupied by Elder R.C. Porter, who presented the subject of "Bible Sanctification," as introduction for criticism and questioning.

The next was a sermon by Elder A.T. Jones. He said:

AN INTERESTING DISCOURSE

THE SUBJECT OF THE LESSON WAS THE CHURCH as the house of God, bringing together those texts which speak of the church as the body, etc. "The first I call attention to is 1 Timothy 3:14–15 which calls the house of God the church of God, and the object of Paul's writing in this particular place was to show us how to behave ourselves in the church, a most important study and, for want of knowledge on this point come many of the church difficulties, but I read the text to show that the house of God is the church of God. Now reading Hebrews 3:6 we find that we are Christ's house, and the chapter shows how faithful Christ was over His house, the subject opening in the second chapter, and He is set before us to consider that He was faithful. Moses was faithful as a servant, but Christ was faithful as a master, and in being so He wants us to be faithful in the house of God, as servants to Him who has called us—faithful in everything, verse 17. Paul showed Christ as coming as Adam did, and made perfect through suffering and being tempted that He might save us when we are tempted—doing all this that we in His strength might triumph; by Him and Him alone we can be faithful. Christ met every temptation that we will have to meet and our faith, putting Him in the place of every temptation, we have His strength to overcome and be faithful.

"1 Corinthians 3:9 states that we are God's building. There is not a proper view in the world of what the church of God is and the relation of members to it. It is often said, 'I can be as good a Christian out of the church as I can in it,' but this is not so. No one can separate himself from the church and be a Christian, because such a one is out of Christ. In 1 Peter 2:1–4, 5 this is carrying forward the idea of Paul and in addition that it is a spiritual house being built up of lively (living) stones–Christ being the living stone, and we living by Him are, through Him, made living stones. In the same way the commandments are called 'the lively oracles,' being the law of the living God. Now by coming to Him and becoming living stones having life given free, we are built a spiritual house.

"Further along a living stone is called precious, living stones giving light and capable of being polished so as to reflect an image. The Scriptures carry that very idea of Christ, a precious stone set before all the people, and we, looking at Him, see ourselves and, looking upon His perfection, become like Him and are built up into Him. This idea is followed in 2 Corinthians 3:18, we looking upon the Lord as into a looking-glass are changed from glory to glory, into the same image. The idea is again referred to in the fourth chapter, verse 6. The same One who made light out of darkness in the beginning has shined into our hearts and changed us into His own image. Christ, then, is the living stone, coming to whom we are built up a spiritual house. 1 Peter 2:6–7. Can we all say that we believe in Him to that extent that He is precious to us? We ought to so believe. The Scripture Peter refers to is Isaiah 28:16.

"Now see 1 Corinthians 3:10. Here, then, is the foundation, that living precious stone, and we as lively stones are built upon that foundation, a spiritual house. Now read Ephesians 2:19–22. We have here the building thus far. Christ the cornerstone, the prophets the foundation, and we build upon these. In Him the building is fitly framed together (not being living stones before coming to Him) groweth unto a holy temple in the Lord. That is what the church is and we builded for a habitation for the dwelling place of the Lord. When we get such a view of the house of God, is not a membership in it of more importance than we realize? If we can not live peaceably in His house on earth, can we expect to do so in the house hereafter? Now we see by the expressions in 2 Corinthians 6:16 and 1 Corinthians 3:16 that we are the dwelling of Christ, so then Christ dwelling in us and we in harmony with Him, Christ dwells among us by His Spirit. In the book of Revelation, we have the city of the New Jerusalem presented to us, the foundations being of the most precious stones, the most precious one being the jasper. Who is called the most precious stone in our spiritual house? Christ, clear as crystal. Above all these is built the wall of colored stones and above this the jasper stone again, and the glory of God showing through (for God will dwell there), and not needing the sun, although it shines seven times as bright as it does now. How far then can this city be seen on the new earth? As far as vision will extend. Now we have a simile of this in the holy temple of God in the church. Christ as the cornerstone of jasper, the apostles and we as the wall and Christ with His glory shining out of His face to us above it all. Now we are the light of this world as a city set on a hill. Let us read Matthew 5:14 and then Philippians 2:15. Then we should not murmur or dispute. We must be blameless and harmless before we can be Christ's children and stop murmuring or disputing. As a city set on a hill, our light should so shine that it can not be hid any more than the glory of the new city can be in the new earth. And a church composed of such members is what Christ will have soon here, a church which nothing in this world can hide and on which the people will see the glory of God—a church to which all honest people will come as doves do to open windows. There can not be therefore, brethren, anything more sacred out of heaven, and if we look upon it as anything less than this we fail to appreciate it. Let us, then, never again have as common view of God's building and habitation."

Following this came the daily class study on reporting and preparing articles for the newspapers, in which nearly all on the camp ground took part, and then came the regular evening sermon on 'The Evils of Religious Legislation," by Elder A.T. Jones. The speaker began by saying:

RELIGIOUS LEGISLATION

"TONIGHT I WILL NOTICE FIRST THE DEFINITION OF CIVIL: 'Pertaining to a city or state, or to the relation of a citizen to a city or state.' Government we call civil, and its laws civil laws. What, then, can any civil government rightly have to do with anything pertaining to God? The government pertains wholly to earthly things, to man related to his fellow man or to the state. By the very definition no government has anything at all to do with God or religion. Religious acts are religious, civil acts civil. Now, as my subject is civil government and religion, let us define religion: 'The recognition of God an object of worship, love and obedience.' There is a deeper meaning, however. All nations have had some form of God, which they worshiped and honored. There are infidels, of course, but they are known only where the true God has been presented, and not known among heathens. The better definition, therefore, would be, 'The recognition of a god.' Another definition is 'man's personal relation of faith and obedience to God.' These two define religion, now then, what can any government have to do with religion? What is it to you whether I love, honor, or obey God, or not? What harm does it do you if I do not? What can any company, or government, have to do with it? Nothing at all. And the definition of civil deprives government from having anything to do with religion. And that is what the Scriptures teach.

"Turn to Matthew 22:15–23. Now Caesar was the head of the Roman government—of the whole world—and so when Christ said, 'Render unto Caesar the things which are Caesar's,' He meant the civil government. What was to be rendered to Caesar? That which was God's? No, for He said, 'And to God that which is God's'—making a clear distinction between those things that belong to God and those things that belong to Caesar. Are there things that belong equally, or partially, both to God and to Caesar? If so, where are we to make the separation? We cannot do so unless the distinction is clearly defined. Now mark what the Pharisees came to do— 'entangle Him in His talk.' If these are those things that belong both to God and Caesar, then they did entangle him—but no—they left Him convinced they had failed.

"When they admitted the coin was Caesar's they admitted that with which they came to entangle him. Christ went further yet and told them to give God what belonged to Him. So we are to render God what is His, but not through Caesar, and without Caesar. The bill in the last Congress claimed to be one for the better observance of 'the Lord's day.' Now let us ask then, whose image and superscription does it bear? Why, they will say, it is the Lord's! Then what has Caesar to do with it? And if it is the Lord's, then Caesar is robbing God of His day, is he not? Then again, the Sabbath they say is to be observed by civil process. Now then, how can a religious institution be observed civilly? It must be, and can only be observed religiously. Christ's word is against the making of any laws in reference to the Sabbath, or any other religious legislation. A number of states have statutes against morality, or moral offenses, and also statutes forbidding offenses against God. Now they have no right to have such laws. It places them as guardians over the Lord. How also are they to know what is or is not an

15

offense against God? What has government to do with offenses against religion! It makes government partisans in character.

"Now for a government to attempt to punish offenses against God is to have heathen states. Heathen governments had to enforce observance of worship toward their gods because the gods were not capable of taking care of their own honor; but God is fully capable of taking care of His. Our states have upon their statutes books heathen enactments contrary to all Christian principles. To such, the reading found in Judges 6:25–32 will be a good study. These courts that attempt to punish offenses against God argue just as did the worshippers of Baal. They may learn wisdom from Joash's answer. These states usurp the prerogative of God in attempting to punish offenses against Him. Offenses against religion include blasphemy, which is to speak disrespectfully against the established religion, and there are statues punishing such blasphemy. But every man has a right to speak so against any religion. Jesus, the apostles and all Christians have had to do so. And if the statues of Pennsylvania, New York and other states were controlling all, it would not have been possible to have spread Christianity, because it is necessary to speak against the accepted religion in order to establish it.

"Another definition here is morality, 'The relation or conformity of an act ... to the divine law.' And the definition of the divine law is 'obligatory on conscience.' If these statutes have to do with morality they have to take cognizance of man's conscience. 'The moral law is summarily written in the decalogue.' Now this law does take cognizance of the conscience. If then their state is to enforce morality and punish for immorality, it has, according to our Saviour and the apostle John, to punish a man for thinking impurely or hating another. Can states punish where no outward act is committed? Certainly not. Then how can governments take cognizance of morality? God alone can judge in such matters. A government cannot move against such a man until he becomes uncivil, and take charge only of civility, and not morality. I do not attack the statues, but the heading and wording, using morality to define civility. States punish crime which is the outward act, and sin God punishes, being the thought of the heart.

"A crime or breach of justice is a deed of the individual, which the state returns upon the head of the individual,... but a sin is a breach against holiness, and utterly refuses to be measured... and cannot be atoned for by any finite action," is part of a lengthy quotation by the speaker. "Crime is known to government but sin is known alone to God. Crime is not mentioned in the Bible, crime being a civil breach—sin is that which God supervises. The papacy claims to be a moral government and to supervise the thoughts of man, and to find out the thoughts they had to establish the inquisition, and this belongs to every government that attempts to take cognizance of morality. The Inquisition was always carried on to save men's souls, not to punish them. Now the Constitution of the United States embodies the principles of Christ when it says Congress shall make no law respecting a religion, so that provision utterly prohibits our government from making any law to enforce religious observances."

The speaker then read from Bancroft's history of the U.S. in reference to the perfect liberty in religion introduced by Christ and its contamination by Roman government making it national, circumscribing it, and forcing a change in its character. Until the United States was freed from its contamination and reestablished its true nature, being the only government in the world that is in harmony with Christ and the Scriptures, and should ever be maintained inviolate, yet, there are people in every state, Kansas included, that are doing their best to obtain a change of the Constitution to establish a national religion. Just as soon as such a thing is done religious freedom in our country becomes a thing of the past. The speaker then went onto show that the constitution of the United States did not protect a citizen of a state from religious legislation in the states. It only protected an American if in a foreign country, but every state can make all the laws it pleases. This is why Utah is not admitted because the Mormons would establish theirs as a state religion. Congress should prohibit states from making such laws, and so the effort should be to lift the Constitution of the states up to the level of that of the United States.

AT FOREST PARK

Campers Increasing In Numbers And The Exercises Growing More Interesting

The Citizens of Ottawa Flocking to Hear Elder Jones' Evening Lectures—His Definition of "the Powers that be"—Synopsis of the Class Work, Lectures and Sermons—Visitors much Interested in the Book Tent—Mrs. E.G. White Expected soon.

Special Correspondence of the CAPITAL.

FOREST PARK, OTTAWA, KAN., MAY 7...

THE HIGH WINDS AND DUST MADE LIFE at the opening of the meeting some-what disagreeable, but the campers have now made their quarters more condonable and the work of the institute in session is progressing favorably. Over 350 ministers, licentiates, Bible workers, officers of churches and other teachers, with their families, are already on the grounds, and, with the visitors, fill the assembly room uncomfortably at most all the conventions. Nearly everyone carries tablets and pencils and full notes of all the class exercises and reports of sermons and lectures are taken, those attending being better able to do this now, because of the instruction received daily in the reporting class, to which all on the ground, nearly, now belong. Below we give reports of the day's work.

The second session of the institute class showed an increase in member-ship and interest in those who attended. The subject of "Evils of Religious Legislation" was continued, the basis from which governments acquire their just powers, as elucidated in the lecture of the previous evening, was further discussed. It was demonstrated that no government has any right to interfere in any way with a man's exercise of his religion, or to legislate in reference to it–even though a religion may necessitate the sacrifice of a human life. The state in such a case can prevent the human sacrifice because it is an uncivil act, and if committed can be punished for murder under the civil law forbidding murder, but it can not legislate to forbid the man from exercising his religion, nor can his religion come into question in any court of law.

The very parties who argue for a Sunday observance law and its religious observance realize this fact, and in applying for a law ask for a civil observance of the day, as courts can not legislate on religious questions. It was further shown that governments can not afford to legislate upon Sunday laws because it binds men who do so to forever surrender their right to believe. The great mistake made is that they fail to see man has no right to legislate in favor of what he believes, as well as not to legislate against his belief–or in other words that true religious liberty is the assertion of other people's right to believe what they please. A man has no right, of course, to be an infidel, but he is responsible alone to God. If he chooses to be an infidel, he has, so far as government is concerned, the right to be one, or anything else he pleases. Sunday legislators assert their right to keep Sunday, but wish to force their neighbors to do so also, yet think they are asking for religious liberty, but if successful, this enforcement of their views upon others can be only tyranny or despotism. The W.C.T.U. wanted us to agree to help them get a Sunday law and then they would give us an exemption clause–that is, "you help us to fasten Sunday upon others, and we will exempt you," but this would be toleration simply, not religious liberty.

The Bible class that followed investigated the subject of Bible work, it being the object of these meetings to learn how best to carry Christ's message to the world. The meeting was then taken in charge by Elder Shireman, the head of the mission at Kansas City, MO., and the class spent an hour in the discussion of the best methods to interest the world in seeking truths that are vital to our times.

ELDER JONES' ADDRESS

THE AFTERNOON'S ADDRESS WAS BY ELDER A.T. JONES, who called attention to Colossians 1:24, the subject being "The Church, the Body of Christ."

"Next turn to Ephesians 1:22,23 showing the church to be the body of Christ, He being the head. Now we are members of His body in being members of the church, 1 Corinthians 12:27. Turn now to Ephesians 5:30 where it is more strongly stated. Now, brethren, is it a common thing to be a fiber of Christ's body, His flesh, His bones? Read from the twenty-third verse and the closeness of the connection between the church and Christ. Another passage, Ephesians 4:15,16, compares the church and its members to the compactness of the members, joints and bones of a human body, all working in harmony under the guidance of one will, to do the work for which it was created. Again, Colossians 2:18,19 follows out the simile to show the completeness and closeness of the union of the various parts. In Colossians 1:18 Christ is shown to be the head of the body, which is the church. Then 1 Corinthians 12:12,13 shows the harmony that should exist in the church, that all, working together in the place assigned to it, and all guided by the head, its purpose may be fulfilled, as it is stated in Romans 12:4,5.

"In 1 Corinthians 11:12 Christ is head not only of the body, but every member of the body, every man. No man is the head of any other man, but Christ is head of everyone and all. Then how many of the members of the body can perform an intelligent action independent of the head? None then in the church of Christ can perform an intelligent action unless guided by the will of Christ. Then should not every member seek always to be utterly submissive to His will that all they do should be directed by the will of Christ? When such a condition prevails in the church there will never be any room for contention or division among its members. The unity that Christ intends should prevail, will prevail and to such a condition the church must come, and will come soon, as there is work to be done and done quickly, and the work cannot be properly done unless the church is harmonious.

"In 1 Corinthians 12:14 and onward we find that none should murmur whatever position they may be placed in, but each finding his place, should keep it and perform his duty there, not seeking to work independently of others, but harmoniously and helpfully, one towards another, that the will of Christ may be done in the locality where the church may be. God has placed each member in his place, as it has pleased Him, to do through each, in the place they occupy, the work He has to be done there, even the more feeble being necessary. We cannot slight the weak ones, but must bestow upon them more abundant honor. We clothe our body to adorn it and make it more pleasing to the eye, but the face being the expressive feature we leave exposed as it needs no adornment. All then, being united, suffer and rejoice together. Further, if any member is injured, what part feels it the most? Is it not the head? Then when you or I cause pain to a member of the church who do we most hurt? Is it not Christ, the Head? Can we, then, if we love Christ, cause Him to suffer? 'If we slight a weak brother, pass him by, refuse to pity him, the Lord will leave us some day, to find out that there is in us, as great a weakness as we despise,' says Mrs. White, 'in the one we passed by.' Reading Hebrews 13:3 we find the same thought—that all suffer or rejoice together—so then if one member is exalted all should rejoice, aid and cooperate with him. If Christ's will prevails this will be done. An envious man is unfit for any place, because 'he who envies another confesses his own inferiority.' If one is occupying an inferior position acceptably he is following out the will of Christ as fully as if he occupied the most prominent position. When the church becomes harmonious, all church trials will disappear, and Christ will have only to make known His will and perform the work He has to be done in that place, in spreading abroad the truth, and saving souls in that locality."

THE EVENING SERMON

THE EVENING SERMON WAS ONE OF THE REGULAR SERIES of the expositions of the evils of religious legislation, by Elder A.T. Jones who in opening said:

"Tonight the subject is the powers that be and the limitations upon them. I call attention to Romans 13:1—assenting the powers that be to be ordained of God. This is a comment on Matthew 22:21 referred to last night. 'Render unto Caesar the things that are Caesar's and to God the things that are God's.' By this expression the Savior recognized that those are things due civil government, but he did not define the limitation, yet Paul does do so. I will refer briefly to some portions of the chapter. The question before the Savior was the matter of tribute, so Paul speaks of the same rendering tribute to whom tribute is due. 'Let every soul be subject unto the higher powers.' Titus 3:1,2 tells us to be subject to powers, to obey magistrates etc.; 1 Timothy 2:14 admonishes us to pray for such officers; 1 Peter 2:13–17 urges us to submit ourselves to ordinances that we may be examples of well-doing to others. But do these Scriptures embrace everything, or is there a limit to it? Shall we obey when the commands are contrary to the precepts of God? Turn to Acts 4:17–21 and we find that when the apostles, Peter and John, were brought before the Jewish council and forbidden to preach Christ, they answered 'Whether it be better to hearken to thee, and not to God, judge you.' Now verse 21 compared with chapter 5:28,29 shows that when they were released they went at once to teaching and performing miracles, were again arrested, and when asked if they had not been forbidden to teach, answered, 'We ought to obey God rather than man.' Very well, then the power given to government is limited, and when it conflicts with the commands of God is not to be obeyed.

"Turning back to Romans 13, from verse 7 onward, we find this, that the limits of power of government is defined. Paul knew that there were ten commandments, yet after quoting five of them he says, 'If there be any other commandment it is briefly comprehended in this saying, namely, thou shalt love thy neighbor as thyself;' he knew there were four others defining our love to God, summed up in this, 'you shalt love the Lord thy God with all thy heart, with all thy soul, and with all thy might.'

'Now why did he not mention these four? Because he was writing on the powers that be, and that which pertains to the relations of man to his neighbor, and that governments cannot go beyond this limit-this is civil government, just as I defined it last night. The Lord, then, has set this limitation on civil government: 'Thou shalt love thy neighbor as thyself.' Now if we remember what Paul is writing about we see why the first four commandments are not mentioned–because they pertain to our allegiance to God, and have nothing to do with our duty towards civil government, and no government has a right to interfere with our duty to God. Paul is defining the limits of temporal power, and if a Christian obeys the commands of

God, Caesar will never have a fault to find with him, (for Paul is writing to the Christian church at Rome, remember, and not to the government) so all Caesar would have to do with such a people would be to collect the tribute. The Constitution of the United States recognizes this principle.

"In Jeremiah we find that Nebuchadnezzar was raised up by the Lord to destroy Jerusalem and take the Israelites captives in Babylon for seventy years at the commandment of the Lord. Numbers 3:26–29 shows that the Lord promises the Chaldeans shall take Jerusalem and carry the people captive. There are abundant evidences of all of this. Now then, this king had been made the power to the children of Israel, by the Lord Himself, yet when this same king tried to force the brothers of Daniel to worship an image of his creation, and upon their refusal were cast into the burning fire, yet the Lord Himself rescued them. If then, the government, represented here by the king, was to be obeyed in all things, because ordained by God, why did the Lord rescue those who disobeyed, standing by them and sanctifying their disobedience? Is it not because the limit of the powers he is confined in many relations to his neighbor?

"But now let me turn to another phase found in the third commandment embodied in states forbidding the violation of this commandment. Now when the Lord tells us not to do a thing the only safe way is to obey unquestionably. No power then can legislate on the third commandment, yet in opposing such legislation it looks as though we were favoring blasphemy, and sanctioning it. Blasphemy is wrong in every phase of it, but it is a wrong that civil government can have nothing to do with, without involving other evils and opening the way for oppression and despotism. If governments can legislate on one commandment why cannot it legislate on all, and usurp all the privileges of God, establishing a theocracy on earth and shutting out God entirely?

"Legislation against murder, theft, and other crimes are not based upon the commandments of God. Nations legislated on such crimes before the commandments were known to them. Civil governments legislate on these matters independent of, and without reference to, the commandments. It is inherent in man to protect himself and his family against criminal attack. Enactments against crimes grow out of man's relation to his neighbor, and not because the principles are defined in the commandments, and are not enforced as commandments of God, because it would force governments to go into the thoughts of man. Tomorrow night I shall consider the statues against blasphemy."

AT FOREST PARK

Mrs. E.G. White Arrives And Takes Part In The Good Work

The Morning Talks of Great Interest-A Large Attendance—
Arrangement for Sabbath School Exercises
—The Lecture on Evils of Religious Legislation.

Special Correspondence of the CAPITAL

FOREST PARK, OTTAWA, KAN., MAY 9...

A.T. JONES' SERMON

YESTERDAY, AT THE MORNING HOUR, the subject discussed was civil government and religion—civil defined as man's relation to a city or state, and religion as man's recognition of a God, the Savior recognizing this distinction when He said: 'Render unto Caesar (civil governments) the things that are Ceasar's, and unto God the things that are God's.' Morality belongs to God, being conformity to the divine law, which men admit to be the Ten Commandments, the supreme rule; so morality is due to God, the Author of the law. Hence, civil government can have nothing to do with morality. It is necessary, then that all should have a clear understanding of this distinction. A sense in which the courts, for instance, use the word, conveys a wrong impression. They speak of offenses of morality, meaning good manners, but that is a perverted sense, covering the ground of immorality. It would be better for the courts to adopt another term to express the idea they wish to convey. Uphold then, always the correct definition, conformity to the divine law. All else is immorality. If courts would legislate on civility only and prohibit in civilities, leaving morality to God to whom it belongs, men would have a clearer idea of their obligations to God and government. All the confusion existing because of this misuse of the term comes from the papacy, the combinations of church and state (which will come into a succeeding evening lecture) by which a theocracy, a moral government of God upon the earth, was established with all its train of evils and horrors. All the errors come from this, and it is almost impossible to have the courts see this and take advance steps rising above it, confusing all distinctions, mixing divine and human things in almost inextricable confusion. Now, conformity to the divine law does not consist inaction only, it lies in the mind 'with which we serve the law of God.' Now the reformers propose to make the Ten Commandments the law of this country. Then they must compel all men to comply in thought with this law. How can they ascertain the thoughts? By confession only? How alone can they compel confession? By the inquisition. But, if they make the divine law the civil law of the land and go only as far as civil law can go, that is, taking cognizance of actions only, then they make the commandments supervise the actions only, and that the divine law is to be satisfied with outward observance only. Does this not bring it down to the condition of things in the days of Christ? Let us read Matthew 15:1–9, a nation of hypocrites outwardly moral but inwardly polluted-white sepulchers. If these reformers would use the gospel and convert men inwardly then the outward observance would be in conformity with God's law.

"Men can never be made moral by law, but bigoted men never learn by experience; ambitious men will ever attempt to force others to conform to their ideas of propriety. Now it is a fact that all men are immoral; immorality is sin and sin is transgression of the law. 'All men have sinned and come short of the glory of God.' 'By the deeds of the law shall no flesh be accounted moral in his sight.' Hence, by the law no man can be made moral. As immoral man cannot keep a moral law; it takes a moral man to do that. Now the morality of God is witnessed without the law, being made manifest through Jesus Christ, through whom alone men can be made moral. Otherwise there would have been no need of a Savior. What then can be accomplished by men, for morality, through law? Further, if men, having the moral law (the best one God could give them) become immoral, is it reasonable to argue that men can pass a finite law that will make men moral? There is then no morality in the world except through faith in Jesus Christ; so then we cannot separate morality from the religion of Christ, and as religion belongs alone to God, government having nothing to do with religion or morality, why it can have nothing to do with the morality of man. It requires divine power to secure morality. It is the work of the Holy Spirit to write the divine law in the heart and lay the foundation and principles of morality. Now the church is God's means of presenting morality to man, but it is not the office of the church to enforce it or punish immorality. It is the office of the church to persuade men to come to Christ and obtain, through the Spirit, strength to keep the law. When one lapses from morality its office is not to punish, but 'to restore such an one,' and persuade him to turn again to Christ. Here is where the papal church failed, attempting to punish for immorality, instead of turning the sinner again to Christ. Here is just where the church turned from the right path and landed in the papacy, and if the right of the church to take this step is admitted, then all the rest must logically follow, so that when men seek again to take this first step all the results that culminated in the papacy must logically follow."

The Bible reading that followed, given by Elder K.H. Porter, the subject being "The Kingdom." He called attention to the expectation of the W.C.T.U., that a theocracy was to be established here upon the earth, and said this reading is prepared to answer the assertion that the kingdom was set up in the time of Christ.

❖

To what are Christ's people invited at His second coming?
Matthew 25:34
❖

When was this kingdom founded?
From the foundation of the world
❖

What do we read about this?
Genesis 1:26
❖

What were they to have?
Dominion
❖

What is dominion?
Authority, ruling
❖

How extensive was it to be and who the king?
All the world, and Adam the king
❖

Did man always retain possession?
Hebrews 2:5–7
❖

How was it testified?
David in Psalm 8
❖

Were all things put under Him?
No
❖

Has man, then, lost dominion?
Yes
❖

What covenant did God make with His people?
Exodus 19:5–8
❖

25

What was promised here?
The Jewish theocracy; Jeremiah 11:24

❖

Did the Jews afterward reject God as their king?
1 Samuel 8:1–4; 10:19

❖

Did God reserve the right to choose a king for them?
1 Samuel 8:22; 10:24

❖

And did not God choose David in Saul's place?
1 Samuel 15:28

❖

What promise did God make to David?
Psalm 89:34–39
(The throne, then, of David was to be established forever.)

❖

How long did the descendants of David reign?
2 Chronicles 36:11–17

❖

Why was the last king, Zedekiah, rejected and the people
carried captive for seventy years?
Ezekiel 21:21–27

❖

Upon their return did they appoint a king?
No. They afterward were subject to other nations

❖

Are any of David's sons still living to take the throne?
Acts 2:29–32

❖

Who is this?
Christ

❖

What did the angel Gabriel have to say in regard to this?
Luke 1:31–32

❖

Did Christ take the kingdom while on earth?
John 6:15; Luke 19:11

❖

Must He go away and come again first?
Luke 19: 11–15

❖

What does Christ say of His Kingdom?
John 18:36
(The W.C.T.U. wants to make Him king by voting Him in.)

❖

Did Christ restore the kingdom while on earth?
Acts 1:6

(Christ's kingdom, then, is not of this world, was not set up when Christ was upon this earth, and no human power can set it up.)

❖

What was Christ's office on earth?
Deuteronomy 18:18

❖

Who was this Prophet?
Acts 3:22

❖

What office does He hold in heaven?
Hebrews 8:1

❖

How long will He remain there?
Psalm 110:1

❖

Where is Christ's throne?
Psalm 11:4

❖

Will Christ have a separate throne from the Father?
Revelation 3:21

❖

How long will Christ remain on the Father's throne?
1 Corinthians 15:24–28

❖

How long will He sit upon David's (his own) throne?
Luke 1:33

❖

Are there not then, two distinct thrones?
Yes

❖

When do Christ's foes become His footstool?
Psalm 2:7–9, Revelation 19:15, 16

❖

When will this be?
At His coming

❖

In connection with what event is this?
Daniel 7:9, 10; 13, 14

(The Father sits upon His throne and Christ is brought before Him and crowned king at the judgment. This is why it was necessary for Christ to go away to receive His kingdom.)

❖

What are Christ's titles at that time?
Revelation 19:16; 14:14

❖

What becomes of earthly kingdoms then?
Revelation 17:15–18
*(When the kingdoms of this world cannot become Christ's, when
the national reform movement succeeds, but only at the judgment.)*

❖

What is done with the earthly kingdoms then?
Daniel 2:35–44

❖

How long will Christ's kingdom last?
Daniel 7:27

❖

Where is the kingdom to be located?
Daniel 2:35

❖

What then will Christ say to His people at that time?
Matthew 25:34

❖

What kingdom was prepared in the beginning?
Genesis 1:25

❖

Who will set it up?
The second Adam

The lesson by Elder Jones for the afternoon was a continuation of yesterday's, being further illustrations of the membership in Christ's church.

"Let us consider Romans 14:13; we are not to judge one weak in the faith to find fault with him, judge or dispute about his weakness, but, as we shall see, to strengthen him. Bearing in mind our relation to Christ and to one another, Christ being the head, if any are injured He feels it the most, and therefore if we love Him we will not hurt one another. If we are cruel to one another we fail to appreciate the love of Christ. There are other things also we can not afford to do, lest we offend and hurt Christ. In 1 Corinthians 8:1, 4–13 is presented before the great field of knowledge as the Lord presents it, and we may think we understand a subject fully, yet continued study shows us our lack of knowledge. Everyone does not know fully that there is but one God, and their conscience being weak, is defiled, and does those things he should not, being still contaminated by old associations, yet the eating of meats and such things does not commend us to God, but beware how you act, lest others may be turned away from the truth, by the assertion of your rights, because of the knowledge you have. If by your assertion you cause a weak conscience to follow what he may think to be right he may be lost. We should have a guardian care over one another, and not do aught that would cause a brother to stumble, but be tender and careful not to do anything that would cause your weaker brother to do wrong. In 1 Corinthians 10:23–33, Paul says, all thing are lawful for him, but all things are not expedient or do build him up. Go where you are called by duty, asking no questions, unless you are told by the one inviting you of the wrong, then refuse, not for your own sake, but for his sake who is weak and does not know the wrong he commits. If he knows that you make no distinction between right and wrong, from his standpoint, no opinion of the value of truth you present is weakened. Our brother's good is what we are always to consider, even if all right in itself, that by yielding for his sake we may draw him to a full knowledge of the truth, and he becomes strong like you.

"Romans 14:15 speaks the same way. Am I going to be so careless of my relationship to that person if I love Christ, if Christ died for him? Will we not love every one whom Christ loves? Yes, and that love includes every person in the world. Verses 20 and 21 show that we should do nothing to cause another to fall, and if we do ought doubting its propriety, it is sin, and–our course may lead another to fall and be lost, another for whom Christ died. Now we are not here to judge one another, even Jesus came not to judge but to save men from their sin. In Matthew 7:2, he tells us not to judge another, and Luke 6:37 gives the same record. So then there is nothing of this kind for us to do in this world, until Christ comes, 1 Corinthians 4:5. Daniel 7:21, 22 gives us further particulars as to the time judgment will be given to the saints, so read 1 Corinthians 6:2–4. The reason of all this is that in the new life we shall see perfectly and be able to see the degree of the guilt of the individual, and this is shown in 2 Corinthians 10:5,6, being able to judge only after our own obedience is fulfilled. When will this be? When every thought is in harmony with Christ? How many are there now in that condition? Then none have any right to judge anyone.

"In Luke 6:36 Christ pleads with us to be merciful. Now read James 2:13 with this, because we will be judged without mercy who judge without mercy. Now mercy is treating another better than he deserves; so then if we judge we will be treated as we deserve and not better than we deserve. If God had treated our first sin as it deserved we would not have lived to sin a second time. Or can we grow into the likeness of God if we do so, and in judging another we condemn ourselves. In judging the motives of another we put our own interpretation on his motives, and then condemn him for what we originate in our own hearts, so then in doing this he is guiltless but we condemn the sin of our hearts, hence condemn ourselves. Now see the Scriptures on this point—Romans 2:1. This is a truth and we can never escape it. But even if another does sin can another measure guilt? No; only God knows the law and the motives. When we attempt to judge we place ourselves in the place of God, and make popes of, ourselves. Now James 4:11

shows that in judging we place ourselves as judge in the place of God. So the whole line of Scriptures speaks against the judgeful spirit. Brethren, let us quit it all. The Savior shows another effect of speaking evil—Matthew 5:25, 26. What commandments are broken? 'Thou shalt not kill.' 'Thou shalt not commit adultery.' In this way we pass judgment, and those to be judged are the ones that have passed judgment on another. These things are written for our guidance. Brethren, let us see that they are practiced."

The evening discourse by Elder A.T. Jones on "The Evils of Religious Legislation," was opened by answering a few written questions, and then the speaker said:

"The subject tonight is statutes, enforcing the third commandment under statutes prohibiting blasphemy. I read Judge Cooley quoting from Justice Storey, defining blasphemy: 'Speaking evil of the Deity.' What harm can that do to me? Wherein does that interfere with the rights of his neighbor— 'Speaking evil of the Deity with an evil purpose, to detract from his dignity.' If men speak evil of an idol they rob him of his dignity, but the soul's dignity can not be lessened by anything men can do. Such statutes belong to heathendom but not to Christianity. 'A bad blasphemy but implies something more than a denial of religion—a bad motive must exist.' I heard a minister utter blasphemy from the pulpit but he could not be prosecuted because no bad motive existed. None are prosecuted really, under such laws, except to vent religious bigotry and spite upon someone disliked. 'There must be a willful and malicious attempt to lessen men's reverence for Deity or accepted religion.' Here lies the vital point. Men can blaspheme against any other religion except the accepted religion and this religion is generally the wrong one. Christianity is never popular, or the accepted religion, or seeks to be enforced by civil power. 'Words may be uttered that are blasphemous, but unless uttered with malice they are not actionable.' So then the law has to search the intents of the heart and this they do 'by the nature of the words themselves.' Well then, in a trial by jury sitting in judgment, there are the words uttered–are they uttered maliciously? This is to be gathered from the words, so it is left to the jury to define blasphemy and as juries are made up of our neighbors, it is as Bancroft says it was in colonial times—'The highest crime, or what twelve men decided it to be!' Anyone has an absolute right to lessen men's reverence for the accepted religion, if he thinks it is wrong. Did not the apostles want an accepted religion which men reverenced, and did they not have to lessen their respect for it? Did not the Savior send men forth to do this very work? Did not these men aim directly at this lessening of reverence to their duties? Are not the Chinese duties as sacred to them as ours are to us? Now if their reverence is not lessened what foothold can Christianity ever obtain otherwise? So then have not men the right to do this work? Certainly. If now China banished every Christian missionary would it not be carrying out the principles enunciated by Justice Story and several states having such laws—all of which belong to 'an established religion?'

'The laws against the Christian Sabbath are not so defensible,' says Bancroft, 'but they belong with the laws against blasphemy.' "

The speaker reads from the laws of Pennsylvania to show the character of the law to prohibit blasphemy because of public necessity "to preserve the public tranquility." What else did Rome do in the days of the apostles? It killed them for doing this very thing. Very well, then, Rome was right in killing the Christians. Did not Luther do this very same thing and did not the papacy forbid it? Did not John Huss die for doing this? Was not then the government correct in punishing them? Are not all these laws, then, opposed to the gospel of Christ? Certainly they are. The speaker then read from the same authority to show how the above decisions came about—from a debate in a debating society, one of its members saying "the Scriptures were a fable and told lies." He was fined $50 in order to convince him it was no fable and told no lies. How long would it take, on this line, to convince infidels of the truth of the Bible? He read a decision of Chief Justice Kent to the effect that to revile religion was a liberty against the freedom of free speech, and practically that the reason why blasphemy is punished is because it is an offense against the popular religion. The Christian religion is a denial of the popular religion, and Jesus was accused of blasphemy and would have died for it if they could have sustained it. He exposed and reviled the Pharisees, the exponents of the popular religion, and to them it was "malicious," and they were carrying out the principles of these decisions.

Quotations were then given from Kent to the same effect as Storey and Bancroft. The statutes are not wrong because blasphemy is right, but because the state is attempting to punish a wrong with which it has nothing to do. Mr. Kent admits the statutes were only continuations of colonial laws which established the Sabbath observance, hanging for witchcraft, etc., and further these statutes appeal to the English statutes, which belong to a union of church and state, and not to a republic, where these are distinct. They belong, then, to just that superstitious theocracy of the colonial days, Bloody Mary and Europe.

The speaker then read to this effect again from Kent, who goes to the pagan governments of antiquity and papal Europe to sustain his decision. Why did he not go to the Bible? Because the words of Christ would not have sustained him, although he was trying to base his decision on the principles of the Christian religion. Christ's injunction to "love your enemies" would not support persecutions for blasphemy. These laws came into our country through the papal power, Henry VIII being called defender of the faith by the Pope, and after his rebellion put himself at the head of the Church of England, it being really a papacy, only with Henry VIII at its head instead of the Pope. So the English system is the papacy, only one step removed, and our colonies, being founded on the English laws, form a direct line of statutes back to the papacy and behind all paganism out of which the papacy originated. Such laws should never find a place on the statue books of a free country. These laws, too, were enforced by men who supposed they were not interfering with the belief of any man, even though they prevented a man from saying anything against the accepted religion. What right has a nation to say to anyone, "We don't propose to interfere with your belief," unless they have the means at hand to ascertain what he believes? Does it not imply the inquisition?

MRS. WHITE ARRIVES

Night before last Mrs. E.G. White arrived and occupied the special tent provided for her. Early the next morning she appeared in the social meeting and spoke feelingly to the people. She urged all to lay down their burden of sin, by confession, at the feet of Jesus, and go free in the freedom which Christ gives. She pleaded with them to believe the promises of Jesus to give all weary ones rest who would come unto Him. She asked all who had confessions to make to do so early in the meetings that they might enjoy abundantly of God's blessing. She felt very thankful to God that He had permitted her to meet the Kansas brethren again, and hoped that this meeting would be the most blessed one ever held among them. Arrangements have been made for a daily discourse by this lady which will be at 5 o'clock in the afternoon, beginning today. The evening lecture in the tabernacle was well attended. The storm of the day before had laid the dust, the wind was not uncomfortable and many citizens attended, more particularly because thirty-three young ladies and gentlemen from the camp visited the homes of people, and explaining the nature of the sermons and lectures, invited them to attend.

THE MORNING INSTITUTE...

A. T. JONES SPEAKING

THE MORNING INSTITUTE CONTINUED THE INVESTIGATION of true religious liberty, as given in yesterday's issue. Speaking of the enforcement of morality, the speaker said that there was something the church did enforce, and that was discipline, but not morality. If it had the right to enforce morality, it would have the right to punish immorality. The Lord uses the church to promote and secure morality in the world. If the church independently attempts to do it, the church takes the place of the Lord. The latter works through the Spirit, by which, using the church as a medium, the work is done. "We in Christ's stead pray ye to be reconciled to God." Those things that are bound or loosed on earth are so bound or loosed in heaven, only after all has been done in accordance with the Scripture instruction on that point, else it is not the word of God at all. When the word is followed strictly it is the work of God and not otherwise. This, however, will come in more fully in a subsequent sermon. Bear in mind that the line between the truth and the strongest objection to it is very fine, and to discriminate we must be very close thinkers, yet the Lord has thought them out before us, and given us illustrations in His book to guide us. He, then, has given us the beast and his image to study, and if we realize what the beast really is, we will be able to detect its image. Keep the distinction clear, then, between morality and civility, the first referring to our thoughts, emotions and passions; civility, taking cognizance of outward actions simply, and also to remember the distinction in those things civil that refer to our connection with men and our allegiance to God. If men aggregate together for protection they must respect the property, for instance, of their neighbors. The state forbids stealing, not from a religious standpoint, but a civil sense. If a man worships an idol he is immoral, yet the state cannot class it as such, but as uncivil. If a man steals that is not immorality. Immorality began before. He was immoral before stealing, and when he stole he became uncivil. Immorality demonstrated outwardly becomes incivility. Nothing under the first table of the decalogue can become uncivil unless expressed outwardly. A man having other gods is simply immoral and harms no one, hence it is not incivility, and can not be unless an act is committed that affects another.

The speaker then read from Schaff's Church and stated an argument to show that to speak against the popular religion was to speak against the law, but the trouble is that a state has no right to have a religion, no earthly government having the right to punish offenses against religion or to enforce the observance. The quotation was the following: "To say religion is a cheat is to dissolve all obligations by which civil societies are preserved; and that Christianity is part of the law of England, and therefore to reproach the Christian religion is to speak in subversion of the laws." In reference to speaking against a religion dissolving the civil obligations of individuals the speaker showed that the obligation remained unimpaired no matter what change occurred in the religious sentiment.

THE SECOND ANGEL'S MESSAGE

ELDER D.T. JONES [NOT A.T. JONES; ED.] PRESIDENT of the Missouri conference and secretary of the General Conference, occupied the 10 o'clock hour in the investigation of the "Second Angel's Message," usually thought to be a difficult one to present and not to give offence while showing clearly the essential point which underlies it. It may be that we dwell upon points in its presentation that are secondary and make the primary. After reading Revelation 14:8. "And there followed another angel, saying, 'Babylon is fallen, is fallen, that great city, because she made all nations to drink of the wine of the wrath of her fornication,'" said:

"The fact seems to be in this that the people represented here have pursued such a course that God has been compelled to separate Himself from them, and He asks His people to come out from among them. God's law is the basis of His government, and when a people set themselves up in opposition to His law, they are in rebellion.

"If rebellion is transgression of God's government and is sin is transgression of the His law, in order to get back in harmony with God again, it is necessary to render obedience to God's law. God gives the power to render that obedience through Jesus Christ, and I wish to be so understood in speaking of rendering such obedience. Babylon is a symbolic expression borrowed from Genesis 11, at the building of Babel, and meaning 'confusion,' so we go back to that period to find the inception of this, that results finally in the fall of Babylon. In Genesis 10 and 11, we find that the wicked separated themselves from the righteous in the place of God, and so they spread over the earth, and began to build a tower, one purpose being to build a tower to worship idols and to save them from another flood, and that by reaching the clouds they could learn the reason of the flood. In all this we find every element of rebellion and defiance—open rebellion against the expressed will of God, turning away from the true God and worshipping strange ones. Baal, the main one, opposition to the will of God, is the one which, when fully developed, will separate man from God when they have gone that far. God is compelled to reject them and carry on His work through other people.

"Now I want to trace this element through the Scriptures and see if it does not always so result. The object of God choosing Abraham was to keep alive a knowledge of Himself in the world and preserve a people for Christ. His promise included the exaltation of the people as a nation to be an example to all nations round about them. But their sins frustrated this and God sent them into captivity that in this way His purpose might be carried out. These nations, however, were pagan and idolaters, but the knowledge of the true God was so brought before the king that he was forced to acknowledge Him; yet instead of worshipping Him he turned to his idols and enforced this under the death penalty. Here was defiance against God and rebellion against the law of God, and in doing this he placed himself where God could not reach him. Here was a fall and rejection of the confused mass of paganism that existed in the world at that time. Now coming down to the time of Christ, we find Him and His apostles presenting the true God to the world. Coming down the centuries we reach the papacy bringing in confusion and finally defying God, and compelling men and women to violate the law of God under penalty of death. God then rejected Catholicism and raised up Martin Luther to present the true light. Then we have the fall of Protestantism and its rejection of the Lord. It is through Protestantism that the last message is not to world. [Sic.] We find that Babylon–all false religion–is divided into three parts, we believe to be paganism, Catholicism, and Protestantism. Turning to Zechariah 13:8–9, the same division is brought to view. The last of these three divisions has a searching test applied to it, and through that trial develops a people that calls upon His name. Why does the prophet refer in the text to one division?

"Looking abroad we can see how and where it, the third angel's message, is going. Is there any openings among pagans, or a strictly Catholic country, for the proclamation of the message? As far as I know the message is going to the Protestant population of the world. But cannot others be saved? Certainly, and there has never been a section rejecting it, but paganism, as a great religious system, and Catholicism also, have been rejected of God, and the trial in the last days develops a people from that class that God has not rejected. We expect the fall of Babylon, and the question is when will this be fulfilled? I think it will be when Protestantism turns its back on the law of God and compels men to violate the commandments of God under the penalty of death. Such has been done before, but Babylon exists before it falls, and it may fall before it is rejected of God. Every time it rejects light there is a moral fall, and a partial withdrawal of the Spirit and power of God, but not to that extent that there will be when they finally persecute the people of God and try to compel them to violate the law of God under the penalty of death. Then they will be rejected and God's people called out from among them. Now then the primary, or real point, is not in the fruit it has borne, but that which causes the fall—the rejection itself. The rejection is not to be found so much in the appearance of that people as in the act committed. It is then the rejection that constitutes the fall, and not the results of the fall we see around us."

The afternoon sermon by Elder A.T. Jones was a continuation of the sermons on "Church Government." In beginning the speaker said:

"In Matthew 25:14–15, especially the latter, shows us that God gives to each one of us according to his ability. Now the church is the body of Christ and our membership in it is a membership in Christ's body, and members of one another, the church being as the human body, with Christ being as the head of each member, the head directing each member and His will the will of all, each and all being subject to Christ, and never the will of one controlling the other, which would be putting a human will in the place of Christ. Further the members so controlled would be molded by the human will and not according to the will of Christ. If Christ gave all the ability, all would have to come to Him as to a fountain, but to each one He gave according to his individual ability to use the gift. Now then this one who made two talents out of his two, is as much a success as the one who doubled his five talents. And also Christ has given to every man, no one is an exception. Therefore let none be like the one who had but one talent and thought he was of no particular talent and made no effort. This parable means us. There is something peculiar to each that no one else has. That is what is meant by "His several ability," and it is this personality that Christ uses to accomplish His work here in this world. He puts His Spirit upon that personality and uses it to advance His cause. It is not true then, as some say, that anyone has no influence. All exert more or less influence upon those around them, and often an influence for wrong, so that what we should do is to see that our influence is always for good.

"So then Christ can accomplish with your talent what He cannot do with anyone else. He uses our talents to influence others into investigating the truth. This is illustrated in the preaching of Paul and Apollos, and Peter, one influencing one and another, the next, but God over all, Christ in it all. 1 Corinthians 3:4–8; 1:11–13. All were ministers of Christ, and each one ministered according to his several abilities, and the brethren should have given God the praise. It was the duty of each to make the strongest possible expression for Christ, and each one of us should do the same, because Christ can make an impression by each one that He cannot through any other. So then Christ wants us to be ourselves and no one else. These are those who want us to be ourselves and them also, and others want to be themselves and some one else too. Such destroy their personality and separate themselves from Christ. Scholars and others often unconsciously copy from others."

The speaker used Melanchthon. Luther, Lorenzo Dow, and others, to illustrate how characteristics are used by Christ to certain work that has to be done, and to show that no one should copy after another but all to copy after Jesus, otherwise we catch a human influence and not a divine.

"In Christ is the fullness of all divine influence and if we copy from a human being our work will have a human mold and not the divine. It is necessary then that each one should learn of Christ alone else we will spread a human influence instead of a heavenly. Never, then, copy after another or adopt another's style or peculiarities. If each is left to be impressed by the Spirit of God, all the work will have the divine impress, and be well done. It may not be, and probably will not be done my way but your way, which is the only way you can do it; nor does this mean that you are not to learn better methods, but when you have a better way, the only way you can apply it is in your own way. The Savior said in Matthew 23:8, that there is but one Master, and we are all brethren. Don't ever forget this. James in chapter 3:1 tells us not to strive for mastership. If you do work that does not suit my ideas is it my place to condemn it? If I do, whose place do I assume? Are you responsible to me or Christ? He is your head and not I, and His will is your will. Romans 14:4. I have no right to dictate to another man's servant how his work shall be done. It does not follow that because it is not done as I would do it, that it will not please God. The point is to find out what is the will of God and then perform it to the best of our ability. Christ is the master, His work is to be done according to your ability—sanctifying it unto Himself, and therefore I have no right to make you do things according to my methods, because in this I make myself master. Brethren, let us quit it. 'Be not many masters.' This principle is the correct one and the true one of independence, but it can be carried to extremes and become willfulness. He wants us independent in our originality, but dependent on His will and guidance which will check willfulness and separation. Let there be independence of action, but unity of purpose, all directed by one will and workers together 'laborers together with God.' When this unity prevails the work of Christ will prosper as it never has done before."

THE EVENING LECTURE…

BY A. T. JONES

"WHOMSOEVER THE SON MAKES FREE IS FREE INDEED the Savior said, and in setting them free religiously He set them free in all respects. Slaves were Christ's free men, and masters became Christ's servants. Without religious freedom there can be no such thing as civil freedom. Without liberty in one there can be none in the other. In setting men free the Savior bound them to Him and to God in an allegiance that can not be broken, nor can anything separate from Him. And the disciples were sent into the world to teach this to all the world. But the Roman government filled all the world and its laws said that no man should have any god except those recognized by Rome. The God of the Christians was not admitted by it, and therefore God was a strange one to the government. Another law forbade the introduction of a new religion, under penalty of banishment or death, and Christians in preaching Christianity set themselves in opposition to the established laws which were on the statue books long before there was a Christian. The law was not enacted because of them, and hence they had no chance to call it persecution when they were punished. So that to claim a right to preach Christ was in the eyes of the Romans rebellion against the government. Neander says that, 'the idea of the state was the highest idea of ethics known to the Romans,' and therefore to a Roman what the law said was right. This included all actual realization of the highest idea of good–the highest good a man could accomplish. But to a Christian, in Christianity there was a far superior good that put the Roman government in a secondary place. Now, for anyone to ask Rome to take a subordinate position was treason. The genius of Rome was the supreme deity. The government of Rome derived no dignity or honor from her gods, but from the state itself. Whatever the Roman law said was good could be worshipped, and no other. In conquering all nations and gods, the idea was fixed that the state was supreme, extending even to the Jewish nation and their God. So, when the Christian preached a superior God, it was treason and he became a traitor. The Romans were very jealous about their gods."

He called attention to a fallacious pagan idea or maxim. "The voice of the people is the voice of God. Such a thing can never be. The standard of Rome carried out this idea. The senate and the people of Rome were the voice of God." In quoting from "Civil Government," the speaker read, " 'The more exalted a Roman became the less freedom he had… The whole duty of man was to keep his house in order and be an humble, devoted citizen of the state.' So, then, the religion of the Christian was directly opposed to Roman laws and Christians were necessarily guilty of high treason. Rome could not stand this, and so the Roman empire enforced the law and punished them. Now, if religious subjects are proper matter for legislation, then Rome never persecuted the Christians—she simply enforced the law. So England, and our own country with the Quakers, etc. Enforcement of law is right and cannot be called persecution. If the law was right, killing the Christians was right. But men in this country need not talk against the Romans so long as they seek to make laws for the 'Lord's day' and to enforce the observance of it. The papacy, going on the same principle, enforced the laws simply. All that was done to Huss, when he was burned, was to enforce the law. What we must do is what the Christians did, and that is say that the Roman's law was wrong and they had no right to have such laws. Now did the Roman emperors proceed [sic.] the Christians? Now really did they? He set Rome on fire and laid the blame on the Christians burning them and tormenting them. No pretense of enforcing the laws was made in this case. Domitian banished John to the isle of Patmos, but it was not persecution. John happened to incur suspicion, with many others, and was banished instead of being killed; but it had nothing to do with his Christianity. Domitian's successor undid all that Domitian had done, and, among others, recalled John. The four best emperors Rome ever had—Trajan, Hadrian, Antoninus Pius and Marcus Aurehus—were the ones who persecuted Christians, and it has always been a mystery to scholars. These enforced the laws because they respected them, but the tyrants cared nothing for the laws, hence Christians were left in peace. So, when the laws were broken under good emperors the laws were enforced, but not so under the tyrants. So then the wickedness was not in the men but in the laws which were not such as any nation had a right to have on their statue books."

The speaker then read from Gibbon's History on Rome to show how these emperors enforced the laws and others paid no attention to them, and the letters of Pliny to Trajan asking what to do, and Trajan's reply telling him not to seek after the Christians, but if informed against, the law was to be enforced if they would not obey it. A government has no alternative but to enforce the laws or abdicate. The government did not seek out the Christians but the populace would get up a riot, if any calamity occurred, and it would be blamed to Christians and they would be thrown to wild beasts or otherwise killed. Finally Hadrian issued a decree that no Christian should be accused and all rioters should be held in place of the Christians, against whom nothing should be done except in regular course of law. Antonius Pius did not issue any edict against the Christians but he allowed riots to occur and that brought back the persecution of Christians. But Marcus Aurdius, the best emperor the government ever had, issued a decree to hunt up and destroy the Christians because of his respect for the law. Now these are the only persecutions committed to the time of Decius.

The speaker then read from the same authority in reference to Commodus Caracallas and other tyrants of Rome, to show that none of them persecuted Christians or enforced the law, although filling Rome with the blood of their enemies, Caracalla causing the death of over 20,000 such, and was called "the common enemy of mankind." It may be Christians suffered with others, but not because they were Christians. Then, so far as the emperors of Rome were concerned, there was no persecution of Christians. It all came from among the neighbors, who informed against them, and the law had to be enforced.

The speaker read from his work, "Civil Government," quotations to this effect from various authors to show how impossible it was for a Christian to attend any public gathering, or even witness the marriage of his own daughter, or the funeral of his own relatives, because all ceremonies were in honor of their gods and he could not take part in them, because of such refusals they incurred the hatred of their neighbors so that a Christian was never safe, day or night, being liable to public vengeance at any moment. The iniquity of the thing was in the laws, which gave the people opportunities to complain of, and persecute Christians. When arrested, the magistrates would try to save them, ask them to simply sprinkle some incense on the altar, then they would be forgiven and obtain their certificate. Yet upon their refusal the magistrate would become angry at their "stubbornness" and would punish them to the full extent of the law, practically being put to death for their stubbornness and not for the bribing the law. Some would offer to sell certificates to the Christians which would protect them, and if refused, he would kill them in self protection, that they could not inform against him. But because these men, women and children thus declared their right to worship God according to the dictates of their own conscience, you and I are able to be here tonight to assert our right to religious freedom, a right which men are attempting to deprive us of, and will revive the same spirit of persecution as existed in ancient Rome.

THE CAMP MEETING

A Cloudy Day But A Very Busy One At Forest Park

Elder Farnsworth Not Coming—Mrs. White's Afternoon Address—Many Interested in the Meetings Through Visits of Canvassers—Sermons and Lectures of a Day

Special Correspondence of the CAPITAL

FOREST PARK, OTTAWA, KAN., MAY 10...

A HEAVY RAIN NIGHT BEFORE LAST MAKES WALKING disagreeable and somewhat lessened the outside attendance, yet the afternoon discourse by Mrs. White was well attended, and the evening lecture of Elder Jones on the "Evils of Religious Legislation" called out many from the city. At the early 5 o'clock social meeting, Mrs. White gave an earnest exhortation that touched many hearts, and her discourse at 2:30 in the afternoon we give in full.

Several new tents are being and have been erected since my last, and quite a field of canvas is now in sight. Mrs. E.W. Farnsworth came yesterday and reports that Elder Farnsworth is too much occupied with his duties at the college in Battle Creek to leave.

Special printed lessons have been published for the coming Sabbath school, and it is believed a very successful one will be held.

THE MORNING LECTURE...

A. T. JONES

"THE APOSTLES WERE SENT FORTH TO PREACH THE GOSPEL, and its intention was to gather a people from the world and save them from their sins, and bring them back into harmony with the government of God; so then the basis of the gospel is the recognition of God's government, which is supreme. In

Rome the supreme government was the Roman, and the highest idea was the preservation of the state, and this idea is the prominent one today–that men cannot claim their right to worship God according to their own idea in violation of the laws of the state. Now we know that God has set limitations upon the scope of power of the state, briefly as man's relation one to another. The Roman law forbade the worship of strange gods. 'Worship the gods in all respects according to the laws of your country and compel all others to do the same,' so when men nowadays try to compel men to do this they repeat the same pagan principle. This principle is largely in men now, and when a national religion is adopted it will be a pagan principle (although it is claimed to be Christian); so then we will have a Protestant faith amalgamated to a Catholic. Hence an image to the papacy, a paganized Christianity. Anciently, prophecies were understood after their fulfillment, but the third angel's message is understood in advance, because this warns against the worship of the beast and his image, which is to be a living image exactly like the present. If we will understand and meet it and show the wickedness in it we must understand it thoroughly. To understand a counterfeit it is necessary to study the original. If we study the counterfeit we lose time–to comprehend the image we must study the papacy, the parent and original. Study the making of the papacy and then we will know what the outcome of it, because the people today have to be warned of their danger. Remember, however, that the people will see all this, but they are now taking the first steps that lead to it, but they do not see the danger.

"Now, God has given us the light on this message to warn the people and show them the evil to follow. Before, the church covered the pagan and called it Christianity, so now the same is being done. Well, then, at that time Christians did not respect the established religion, and Rome declared it treason to profess or advocate any new religion, though the laws were framed before Christianity was in the world, so that the action of the Christians was high treason, punishable by death; for the lower classes, of whom the Christians mainly came, Paul saying they were the off-scouring of the world. The Jews also being despised by the Romans, and the Christians were despised by the Jews, so for the despised of the despised to rebel was insolence in the eyes of the Romans.

"When arraigned, they refused to obey and upheld the law of God even unto death, denying that, 'the voice of the people was the voice of God,' and so introducing a new religion. Only one thing was possible by the state–to enforce the law. The state did not wish to persecute, it had to enforce the law. No Christian had any time to call himself safe, and his life was in danger from the emperors (only two of them up to the time of Decius having legislated in reference to Christians), but as every festival and jubilee observance was engaged in to honor the gods, and as a Christian was forced to refrain from everything of the kind, they were constantly exposed to the malice of neighbors and friends who complained of them and forced them before tribunals. The best of the emperors, respecting the laws, had them enforced rigidly, but the tyrants caring nothing of law, left them unexecuted. The wickedness, then, was not in the men who governed, but in the system of laws that gave men the opportunity to persecute.

"The papal church claims that it never put any one to death, that the civil laws were enforced simply, but the laws were dictated by the church, and said to the civil power, execute the papalties or be excommunicated. A man placed above restraint is but one removed from Satan, no matter how good originally, but the glory of Christianity is that the Spirit of God is above all and this restraint, heeded, makes saints. Now if the papal system becomes a national one here, what will follow? Why the laws will be enforced. Take the cases in Arkansas as perfect examples. Let me quote from the argument of the supreme court: 'The appellant's argument, then is reduced to this: That because he conscientiously believes he is permitted by the law of God to labor on Sunday, he may violate with impunity the statute declaring it illegal to do so; but a man's religious belief cannot be accepted as a justification for his committing an overt act made criminal by the law of the land.'

"Here it is distinctly stated that a man's religious belief cannot be made an excuse for disobeying the law. Now this is the pagan principle of Rome, and Arkansas is not behind what other states will be if this system is adopted. This is only a pagan argument and that is all they will see in it. Now for years we have been warning the people this was coming, but they have laughed at us. Now it is being attempted, they will say 'It will never become a law.' When it does become law, 'it will not be enforced,' they will say, and when it is enforced they will argue, 'it is right to enforce the law.' So then, as anciently Christians had to defend the law, even unto death, so will we have to do. They did not work simply for themselves, neither are we to do so. This message given to us is to go to every nation, kindred, people, and tongue. Eminent men will not come to our tent meetings and elsewhere, so they will have to hear these truths from us in prison and from the bench in court—so we will have to tell the people the law is wrong. The Christians never before asked for an exemption clause, neither can we. It would be a sanction of the whole system. It is not our work to ask for exemption clauses, but to hold up the truth against the flood of evil coming. Soon everyone of us will be called blasphemers for saying that Sunday is not the Sabbath, and that the present movement is an image to the papacy, but God has given us the message to the world and that is our work and the power of God will sustain us.

SERMON BY MRS. E.G. WHITE

"'ASK, AND IT SHALL BE GIVEN UNTO YOU; seek and ye shall find; knock, and it shall be opened unto you. For every one that asketh receiveth; and he that seeketh findeth; and to him that knocketh, it shall be opened. Or what man is there of you, whom if his son ask bread, will he give him a stone? Or if he ask a fish, will he give him a serpent? If ye then, being evil, know how to give good gifts unto you children, how much more shall your Father which is in heaven give good things to them that ask? Therefore all things whatsoever ye would that men should do to you, do ye even so to them: for this is the law and the prophets.'—Matthew 7:7–12. We have a promise here from God, and I wish everyone before me would believe it. 'Whatsoever is not of faith is sin,' and if we come asking without faith, if God should bless us we would not recognize or appreciate it. We need a living, active faith, and entire dependence upon God as though we were little children, and then our requests will be granted. 'But,' says one 'I don't feel as I want to feel. I want to feel this way.' This is well enough, and we do frequently have it, but you must not make feeling the criterion of faith, or you will lose many precious blessings. Feeling is not faith. I have sometimes myself felt this way and tried to make terms with God, if He would do so and so, I would do so and so. But, is feeling the emotional part, or is it the oracles of God that testifies to us that we are the children of God? If we show unlimited faith in God, it will lift us up out of difficulties and perplexities. God has said it, and His word is immutable. Come to Him believing He will do just as He says He will. We have it promised that good gifts will be given by our Father if we ask Him. Should we not present our cases then more frequently than we do, and believe He will help us because He knows our helplessness and our want of righteousness and that He must come in and fill us the lack. I want you to know what it is to have a living faith in God. Never can we know the depth of mire from which we have been lifted, only as we comprehend by living faith the length of the cord that was let down from heaven to draw us up–the living chain of mercy He has let down that we must, by faith, cast our whole weight upon, then we can indeed be cured by the blood of Jesus Christ, and His righteousness becomes our righteousness.

"What brought Him to earth to lay aside His royal robes, His crown of glory, His position as one with the Father, clothed His divinity with humanity, and come here to carry on the battle with the powers of darkness in our behalf? Why did He not leave us to do it? Because we had fallen and divine power had to be added to our finite nature to make it successful, to give us any hope of everlasting life. An angel coming could not do the work. How could they understand the work to be done? Christ became a man to sympathize with men. So man, at every step, is overcoming where He did, Christ's work being to show that divinity combined with man could overcome. When Christ came into the world what a work had been going on! Satan had had his own way and man's mind had been clouded so that the precious gems of truth were buried. Christ's first work in the ministry was to gather up these precious gems and rid them of the superstition and tradition that covered them and restore them just as they had been given to the prophets and presented so little children can understand them. This is the work our Savior came to do, and also to represent the Father. Satan had been misrepresenting Him, His work and His Spirit. So then He is a God of goodness, love and compassion. Satan shows Him as a God of justice, visiting the transgressions of the sinners without mercy. When Moses prayed that the Lord might go before him, the Lord said: 'I will make all My goodness pass before thee, and I will proclaim the name of the Lord before thee, and I will be gracious to whom I will be gracious, and will show mercy on whom I will show mercy.' Exodus 34:5, and He also proclaims His own character. After the fall all communication between man and God came through Christ, so we have this presented before us in straight pure lines that if a man will confess his sins, the Father will pardon him. Notwithstanding all this, how few take the lessons home to themselves. Now what are we to do? Why represent Christ here upon the earth, the only way He will be represented. We can go to God for the things we need. Christ has said, 'Enter into the straight gate' and to also 'beware of false prophets.' 'We shall know them by their fruits.' What a man professes is no evidence that he is a child of God, but what he does. Does he manifest a proper spirit? Does he reveal Christ in his home life? Christ revealed the Father. When Phillip asked to see the Father, Christ said: 'Have I been so long with you, yet hast thou not known Me, Phillip? He that hath seen Me, hath seen the Father.'

"Our work is now to teach men how to enter the straight gate, to tell men what they should do to be saved. We want to know what fruit is born, Christ says: 'I sanctify Myself that they may be sanctified.' Have you a home religion? Do you speak kind, true words? Do you make home a place to plead with God and to teach your children to come to Him? That He bought them? Do you teach them, constantly, the claim high heaven has upon them? If so then the precious Savior will save them. 'If I be lifted up I will draw all men to me.' Present before your children that Christ is drawing them and that they are drawing away from Him. Christ is calling them to repentance, not their repenting. No one can repent unaided.

"Christ calls you. How? Did He not erect a cross between heaven and earth? Whenever God the Father and the heavenly train look upon it all bow to it and the angels prostrate themselves before it. Why? Because the plan of salvation has been carried out and the Father accepts it. Midway the cross is erected and sinners are to look upon it and be saved. It is this that brings sinners to repentance. Man may talk of an eternally burning hell, but that does not do the work. It is the love of God. No one can repent except Christ move him. How is it done? Is it a special act for each? It is the Christ of Calvary hanging midway between heaven and earth, and then what? 'Mercy and truth have met together; righteousness and truth have kissed each other.' I plead with God to show me this clearly that I may present to others who have so much difficulty to comprehend that Christ is first and last, the Alpha and the Omega, and has drawn man by a love as broad as the world to Him, and what then? It leads man to repentance and then comes the forgiveness. We want that the brethren and sisters should take hold of this for themselves.

"When Peter had been put in prison, the priests said do not preach in His name, but the angel opened the prison door and bade him to go forth and preach. This was a conflict between the two, and Peter, when arrested said: 'We ought to obey God rather than man,' The love of God, which is beyond comprehension, is constantly drawing men to repentance. It is Christ that is the first and last; the author and the finisher of our faith. Now our faith must grasp this truth. Man's nature is enmity against God. Christ came clothed with humanity and then humanity touched humanity, and by living faith men grasp Christ and repent that they have transgressed the law of God. As they repent He forgives their transgressions. So it is Christ from first to last. Now we want our brethren to see this. What is man to do? Have faith. What kind of faith? To believe that Christ is the propitiation for our sins, and that He brought immortality to light. But what are we to do? Why, this faith is a working faith. Will a farmer fail to sow seed, yet expect a harvest? No more will you unless you are active workers in the cause of God and put to the stretch every muscle, every energy. 'To him that overcometh will I grant to sit with Me on My Throne, even as I also overcame, and am set down with My Father on His throne.' What does that mean? He overcame in our behalf and we are to overcome in His strength. Every evil and defect will shut us out of heaven if we do not overcome through the strength He has given us. Why then groan, 'O, I wish I was a child of God?' If an angel told you would it make it any stronger? You lack faith. Put your faith to the utmost stretch. If I promise you something you would not require an evidence from me. It would be insulting to ask it. Yet we treat God in that way. He says if you ask you shall receive. Now what are you going to do? Ask for what you want. Claim His promise. Tell Him you are weak and cannot overcome unless you have His strength, and that you must have it. Do you suppose you would ask in vain; knock and not be heard? No. If you would have this faith you must be the happiest people on earth. Why? Because you have planted your hopes on these promises and you go on your way rejoicing, knowing He will do exactly as He promised. This faith works by love, and our old hard hearts fall upon Christ and are broken, and He fills us and molds us by His Spirit.

"The trouble with us is that we have never fallen upon the Rock. We are wrapped up in our own self-righteousness. Had we not better believe and mix the truth with faith, having that faith which works by love? Shall we not, in all our connections with each other see Christ in all, and love one another as Christ loves us? Let us take Christ as our precious Savior, and He will be to us a present help in every time of trouble. I am so glad we need not go through life with our heads bowed down looking at our own imperfections. We misrepresent Christ in this way. Have we not everything to be grateful for? Christ has gone to prepare mansions for us. Let not your heart be troubled. Is not that enough to make us glad? Should we not go our way rejoicing, talking of His compassion, His love? Have you, brother or sister, put your mind on the right side of the question? Turn over a page and look over the shadow of darkness to see the love of Jesus Christ. 'Unto us a child is born, unto us a king is given.' God has given us all that mightiness and power. Will we believe He will strengthen us and overcome for us as He overcame? It is humanity combined with divinity that will bring us through the straight gate. Don't dishonor Him any longer by your unbelief. Let us lay right hold of His promise. Open your heart to Him and let self break all to pieces, He will gather you, He will put His mold upon you. The Lord is coming. There is no time for indolence. These is a message to go to the world. We cannot present it to the world if we do not believe in Him. We are receiving precious things. Brethren, will you take hold of this truth; will you by work in your family seek to bring them up in the nurture and admonition of the Lord and carry this spirit into your Churches, so educating yourself that you can preach Christ to them that know Him not?"

THE AFTERNOON SERMON...

BY A.T. JONES

"THE SUBJECT THIS AFTERNOON WILL BE THE GIFT the Saviour puts upon that several ability He gives every man. In several places Paul speaks of that body of Christ, and we as members of that body, and it is always in connection with the gifts of God. I read first in Ephesians 4:3–16 in which the principle is laid down that, 'to everyone is given grace according to every man's several ability.'

"There are the gifts which Christ gives for the perfecting of the saints, perfecting the ministry and the building up of the church. These gifts are not given until man comes into the unity of the faith, and so Paul says endeavor to keep in that unity until we come to the stature of the fullness of Christ. Then when the church reaches that place, the world will see Christ in the church, it representing all the graces and virtues and perfections of Christ— a perfect man completely represented. Then cannot Christ do all He has to do in the world? There is much to be done, and He wants us to come into that unity that the work can be done. 'And if the knowledge of the Son of God,' that we be not tossed about and be deceived. Notice verse 15, dealing with, 'speaking the truth in love.' The margin reads 'sincere' which means in Latin 'without wax.' The honey is squeezed out of the comb and strained and restrained until free from wax, so 'sincere,' being without flaw or stain.

"Now read Romans 12:3–8, the gifts differing according to the grace given to us–all these being gifts of Christ, to all of us. We must realize that each has an ability that Christ wants to use, and so each one should go to

Him to find out his gift and place in the church, then Christ can do the work He has to do in that place through those of His servants who are there. Christ will increase the numbers as the work requires. To each one then has the ministry of reconciliation been given. Being reconciled, you are to tell others that they may become reconciled also. God does not call idlers, but all must be workers.

"Now 1 Corinthians 12: 1–11. The manifestation of the Spirit is given to everyone. Do we believe it? What is it for? To profit withal. Have we so received it? Have we been cultivating it and trying to find out how we can use it to the glory of God and build up the church of God? The gifts, it says, are divided to every man according as the Lord wills, giving the gift and the manifestations of it as pleases Him. Then no one of us is to try to conform our gift to some other man's, each being given according to his several ability. We are brethren, Christ being the master, giving the gifts, being the head, and His will is to move all. Then if Christ gives to you grace according to your ability, and you so exercise it, am I to be envious of you in the exercise of that gift? When we realize that we are equal, and the gifts are given according to our several ability, there will be no place for envying or jealousy. Paul shows here how these gifts are complements one of another, without being absorbed one within another, each complete by all being exercised for Christ, binding all to Christ, as members one of another. Verse 8 gives us wisdom and knowledge. There is a difference between the two. Wisdom is the faculty of using wisely the knowledge that is possessed. Now, if one has wisdom and another knowledge, they, working together to do perfect work. Christ working through both puts His impress upon it, perfecting it. Verse 10 presents the two classes of tongues, one edifies the brethren if another brother arises and interprets it for the hearer, one being the complement of the other."

THE EVENING LECTURE...

BY ELDER A.T. JONES

"THE SUBJECT IS THE MAKING OF THE PAPACY—the union of church and state as it was formed in the beginning and the working of affairs that brought it about. In Constantine's time there were six emperors. Before that there were four, and before that only one was recognized. There were really two, with the others as assistants. Finally, by the death and abdication, it was reduced to two–Constantine and Maximin. From the beginning of the mutual reign of these six men, each strove to become supreme, and each with a powerful army, warring with and killing each other, so that finally Constantine killed the last and reigned alone, but the military power was so equally divided that it became policy to gather all outside power possible. Now Constantine saw the Christian Church just emerging from the persecution of Diocletian, which was not particularly against any denomination (for there were some ninety different forms of Christianity). This persecution, which was the last pagan effort, had united these denominations in self-defense against the common enemy. At this time there was a grasping for power among the bishops of the Churches, and the emperor knew it. Maximin, the emperor with Constantine, made them an offer, but the bishops feared him, but Constantine, being such a consummate hypocrite, won them. In A.D. 311 A party of these bishops visited Constantine and the bargain of support was concluded, they promising him the united support of the church in return for place and power. When afterwards he found how divided the church was, he was extremely disappointed and practically as soon as religion became an imperial attribute, it became the aim of every bishop to curry favor and seek for power from the emperor, so that he never knew again a peaceful day, exclaiming once, O, give me back my quiet days and peaceful nights.'

"Now that being the reason of his conversion from paganism to Christianity, for all the conversion he ever had was a political one. We want to see what the idea of the bishops was in seeking this union. In the church had arisen a false theory of a theocracy, which was the prevailing one in the time of Constantine, and they were determined to turn the Roman empire into a kingdom of God, and so they made themselves dependent on the emperor to gain the power of the secular arm of the government. Now there was originally a true theocracy upon the earth when God led the children of Israel out of Egypt. We all know how the Israelites went down to the Red Sea, Pharaoh tried to follow and was drowned and sunk to the bottom of the sea. Then the Israelites sang the song of Moses and afterwards in the wilderness Moses erected a tabernacle and in it communed with God. This form of theocracy continued until the days of Samuel, when the people asked for a king like another nation, and the Lord chose Saul and afterwards David, and when Solomon reigned in his place, the record is he sat on the throne of the Lord as his father before him, the line being established in David's house by direct promise of God that David's throne would last forever. Zedekiah was the last of the line on earth, being removed by the Lord because of wickedness, and was to remain vacant 'until He came, whose right it is.'

"The next place the throne is mentioned is in Luke when Christ is born, when he is promised 'the throne of His father David.' But He was not a king on the earth—'My kingdom is not of this world'—although born to be a king, so until the next world there can never be a theocracy again. When He died, the people were scattered and the end of the theocracy had come.

"Now when these bishops attempted to set up a theocracy, they turned away from the truth and prevented the purpose of God. Daniel 7 tells that God will not be given His throne until the judgment, so then, any kingdom or form of government of God on earth until Christ comes is treason against God. Now mark what those bishops did in Rome."

The speaker read from Eusebius' *Life of Constantine* to show how those bishops tried to exalt Constantine into a royal selection of God's, a second Moses, to lead the church out of the strange land into the promised land. They claimed that, when Maximin fell off the bridge and sank as a stone was a second drowning of Pharaoh, and that Constantine was a second Moses to deliver the people and church from oppression. Constantine himself followed out this idea to such an extent that he had a tabernacle erected and in it he would go before a battle, and claiming then to have had a vision from God, he would rush out and give orders of the battle, by divine inspiration. So then claiming Constantine to be called by divine appointment, they take the first step in the forming of the theocracy. The next step was to put in a Sabbath to imitate the steps in the true theocracy. This was a natural result, because Constantine wrote them: "Let us have nothing in common with the Jews."

"Under Diocietian, many Churches had been destroyed. Constantine ordered them to be rebuilt and the property restored to them. At that time there was a sect of Donatists who petitioned the emperor to restore their Churches, but Constantine said only the 'Catholic' Churches were to be rebuilt. This brought a series of councils to decide between the Donatists, Arians, and Trinitarians to decide which was Catholic, and so fierce were the disputes and so disgraceful that the theatres parodied the quarrels for the amusement of the populace. Constantine finally placed, in the declaration of principles, the word 'Homoousian' and that decided the fate of all Rome and the Catholic world ever since—becoming the Catholic creed for ever after, so that Constantine prepared the doctrine for this church.

"After the death of Constantine various emperors added additional matter to the creed according to the side of faith they held, causing council after council to obtain unity of belief among the Churches, the emperors keeping the bishops prisoners, when the council would be held, until they agreed to sign the creed prepared for them. At the council of Nice, Eusebius declared that Constantine, when he entered appeared as a god before them, and says: 'One might easily believe that one beheld the type of Christ's kingdom,' and in another place that Constantine's palace was the New Jerusalem described in Revelation by John. Now Eusebius is declared to be one of the best of the bishops. Now if he could see the kingdom of Christ as come in Constantine and his palace, what might the others discover? Constantine's mother sent two of the nails of the cross (claimed to be found) to her son to put one of them in his helmet to protect him, and the other was made into a bit for his horse; and then the bishops claimed this to be a fulfillment of Zachariah 14:20, and that the kingdom of Christ had come. This was the work, and the political scheming, between the church and Constantine.

"Now about his conversion. He was never converted unless on his deathbed. The only conversion was a political one. In 312 he told Eusebius he saw the vision of the cross in the air, of which we have only his own words. In 314 he made a decree that the church donations, and the record

49

is that he could not have given more if he had given to Romans provinces. In about 318 he made the decision of the bishops as fixed as though Christ had done so, provided the person went to them voluntarily. [sic] In March 321, he made the decree to examine the entrails of an animal to decide the cause of public calamities. In 323 he murdered his wife's father. In 326 he murdered his own son, wife and his nephew, and many relatives. In 328 he laid the foundations of Constantinople, 'according to the ritual of paganism.' In 330 it was dedicated to the Virgin Mary, and when finished the statues of pagan deities were all placed in the city; the statue of Apollo was erected in the most conspicuous place. Apollo was the god of the sun worshipping, and was Constantine's favorite god. If, then, anyone can prove he was a Christian it is more than I can do. Constantine caused twelve pillars to be erected, with a vacant space in the center, in honor of the apostles, and also twelve coffins separated as the pillars, for the same purpose, and after his death a new pillar was added and a new coffin for himself, and he shared the worship and honor given to the departed apostles. Can anyone wonder that Paul calls all this 'the mystery of iniquity?"

THE CAMP MEETING

Rain And Mud Tend To Prevent Outside Attendance

Mrs. White Attends the Early Morning Meeting and Speaks Every Other Afternoon—Young Peoples' Meeting in the Big Circle Tent —Many New Arrivals.

Special Correspondence of the CAPITAL

CAMP GROUND, FOREST PARK, OTTAWA, KAN., MAY 11...

THE LAST FEW DAYS HAVE BEEN CLOUDY, with occasional storms, which prevented many from coming to the various lectures and sermons, yet the attendance has been quite good. Mrs. White has decided to speak every other day at 2:30, beginning today. Two sessions of the morning institute are now being held, the interest growing needing this accommodation. Mrs. E.G. White continues to address the early meetings, but will speak in the afternoons at 2:30 only every other day. The large circle tent is now provided with seats and yesterday at the 5 o'clock morning meeting the young people took possession of it, and will hold separate meetings hereafter. Quite a number of new faces are met with and many new tents have been erected. F. E. Belden, instructor in canvassing, is expected Monday. Much regret is expressed that Elder Farnsworth is not to be present.

THE MORNING LECTURE...

A. T. JONES

"AT THE BEGINNING OF THE FOURTH CENTURY the Roman empire was ruled by six emperors and the Christian church, divided into ninety different sects, the bishops of each striving for power. It was necessary for each of the emperors to obtain all outside help possible as the military power was about equally divided. Maximin and Constantine each realized the value of the supposed unity of the Christian church, and so each tried to obtain the support of the Christians, Constantine succeeding. The bishops desired to establish a theocracy, a government of God. There was such a government formerly, actually ruled by the Lord, not directly, but through Moses and the prophets etc. But the people asked for a king and He chose one for them, not abdicating, but still retaining the government, hence it was still the throne of God, and no attempt was ever made by David or Solomon, the Lord promising that the throne should stand forever, in the line of David's house, Zedekiah being the last one on earth, God declaring there should be no other until Christ, the heir, should come again to claim it. Now, then, in a theocracy, it is necessary to have someone to convey the word of God to the people. Now if the Reformers intend to establish a theocracy they must have prophets, so then this will open the way for all the false prophets the Bible speaks of. Dr. Crafts already declares that the preachers are the successors of the prophets to make known the will of God.

"The bishops declared Constantine to be a second Moses, making themselves dependent on him to secure the power of the state to carry out their aims. Now when anyone places himself in such a position he makes himself a tool of the one on whom he is dependent, politicians, as they are now called. Now all the time that Constantine was claimed as a bishop (of externals, i.e. the civil power) and the head of the church, he was never even baptized. Never has there existed so consummate a politician and hypocrite. From 307 to 312 no one could tell what he was—Pagan or Christian, he rode the two horses so well. As the Lord had in His theocracy a sign by which He might be known as the ruler, which was the Sabbath, so the new false one had one also, a counterfeit, not being willing to adopt the original, not wishing 'to have anything in common with the Jews.' So adopting the Sun-day, the day of worship of the sun, the pagan worship was grafted upon Christianity and paganized Christianity became supreme. The Sunday law was passed by Constantine to please the bishops who wanted the power of the government to compel the people to attend church. The first Sunday law compelling the closing of courts, etc. on Friday as well as Sunday is lost, but mention is made of it. The next enforcing Sunday worship is extant. Before these laws the pagans had festival days but no holy days until these laws were passed, so transferring the devotional work of the Sabbath to Sunday they attempt to make the first holy day Rome ever had known.

THE MORNING INSTITUTE

Elder Smith Sharp spoke on the subject of, "The Present Outlook of Prophecy." Prophecy is a part of the Scriptures the Savior taught us to search, John 5:39. I claim that includes all the Bible. 2 Timothy 3:16 shows it to be by inspiration of God. The definition that suits us for prophecy is 'history in advance,' as shown in Isaiah 3, speaking of the events as though they had already occurred. As to how it came, see 2 Peter 1:21, holy men of old, spoke as the Spirit moved them. In another place he argues that they have not followed cunningly devised fables. An intelligent conviction of the prophecies leads us to put in practice the truths they contain. I shall not dwell exclusively on Daniel and John, but they enter largely into the investigation. Ezekiel, in chapter 9, classes Daniel with Job. In Matthew 25 Christ endorses him and his prediction of the fall of Jerusalem. That is sufficient, and further, he is the only one that predicted the year the Savior should be killed, see Daniel 9, in which he gives the date that shall reach to his baptism and death. He being the only one that made these predictions His words add great weight in our investigation of the prophecies. Having seen the fulfillment of many prophecies and there being a few yet to be fulfilled, what is the outlook? How long is it probable, it will take to fulfill the balance? I pass over Daniel 2 and 7, but at the close of this great line of prophecy in Daniel 2, the God of Heaven is to set up a kingdom. We of course believe the ten kings are the existing kingdoms of Europe–the result of the breaking up of the Roman kingdom, to be followed by the fifth kingdom to be set up by the Lord as spoken by James and Matthew, which is this earth made new.

"Now some may question if all these kingdoms are still in existence. Now as they have existed for hundreds of years where is the evidence that they may not exist for hundreds of year longer. Looking at Daniel 11:35 and onward, we find it contains an unfulfilled prophecy. I shall claim as undisputed that the time of the end began in 1798, and shall pass over to verse 40 which all admit is Egypt, pushing at France, and Turkey shall come against the latter. Turkey waging war and, deserted, retreating upon Jerusalem. All then has been fulfilled except verse 45, when the Turk is to be driven out of Europe and retreats to the Holy Land. Now chapter 12:1 here, there can be no mistake that this very time is meant when probation shall close. Christ shall rise up and begin His reign. Now I claim the complications in Europe today are similar to what has been present for years—the 'Eastern Question' being watched, then as now, so what evidence is there that this may not culminate for even fifty years? There are two important events yet to be fulfilled, before Christ is certain to come. The first is the removal of the Turk to Jerusalem and the other is the erection of the image to the beast as introduced in Revelations 13 and 14. The beast we find in Revelation 13, which all admit to be the papacy, the church and state united, which is what the third angel warns against. Why, then, should the message in this last day start out with this warning? Because never before has there been such a tendency of Protestantism to curry favor with the Catholic Church and admit it as a Christian denomination. Now that the second beast is the United States all will admit. We come down then to the warning against the image to be erected to the papacy and against his worship. Now while it may not be the church and state as united in the fourth century, yet it will be religious legislation. I claim that when this occurs, and Sunday observance will be enforced by law, then we say the image to the beast will be complete, and then the time of the end must necessarily be very near at hand. When the people of God will be shut in between the two walls—the decree of the government and the command of God—it cannot take long to finish the question. We have been watching the progress of this movement for years, yet the last effort in Congress may not be repeated for some time, and it takes time to start such a movement again.

"A congressman will generally feel obliged to vote according to the wish of his constituents. Petitions, I do not believe, would influence them, but when the leading people among their constituents undertake to influence them by threatening defeat at the polls if they will not vote as desired, the bill will receive consideration. But now I raise this question, what indication is there that this may not take a great many years and the coming of Christ be long delayed?"

In reply to them several answers were given, from which the following brief is made:

Elder D.T. Jones asked if Turkey, the king of the north, went against France? In verse 40 three powers are introduced, France, Egypt, and Turkey and it is the Crimea war that is the subject of prophecy.

Elder Porter asked if Elder Sharp intended to say that the papacy would come into prominence again. Yes, it is so apparent that all can see it without going to the Spirit of Prophecy. Then how is Daniel 7:26 harmonized with that view? This evidently refers to his temporal power, or dominion, and the judgment, the investigative one beginning in 1844. In a spiritual sense the papacy is increasing, but does not the taking away refer to 1798? Elder A.T. Jones called attention to Isaiah 61:1, "The Lord has anointed me to."

"Why then should we think the day of vengeance of our Lord was preached when Christ came? Because it can not occur until after the day of the Lord comes. I introduce this to show that two events do not necessarily follow because mentioned together, I think the judgment is one referred to in verse 10.

"Jesus illustrates the manners of His coming by the parable of the fig tree in Matthew 24, and gives the signs that the generation seeing them should be living when all was fulfilled. Now the last of these signs was given in 1833, so it cannot be much longer but is not 'this generation" interpreted 'this race' that is the Jews. No; for 'this generation' was not the Jews to whom Christ spake, but the one seeing the signs."

Elder Jones said public sentiment must be moulded as Elder Sharp stated, but will it take a number of years? If we remember that most intense public sentiment is moulded very quickly, it may not take long. Look at the rise of public sentiment in opposition to slavery. For years the abolitionist was looked upon as a criminal, but the sentiment, changing slowly at first, swept away rapidly all over the country. This shows that public sentiment is developed according to the way the subject is introduced. The Sunday movement is in advance of what the slavery question was, and I can see no objections to the soon coming of Christ on this ground.

Elder Rogers said that the fact that the message is going forth is proof that the time is short. This is the fact in other messages, they being always addressed to those who will see the event in the closing scene. To claim the expression "this generation" could not apply to any other is to destroy the force of the application. So we are warned in believing that His coming is "near, even at the door."

Elder Cates called attention to the increased knowledge and rapidity of locomotion in fulfillment of the prophecy that knowledge shall increase and men run to and fro. He illustrated at some length the rise of the sentiment in favor of the abolition of slavery and its spread over the United States; eight years from the time that all three parties had said slavery should remain intact in the states having it, the fourteenth amendment was introduced and accepted by the very men who agreed to the continuance of slavery. Does the cause of the Lord move slowly? I think not.

Attention was called to Revelation 10:7, when the mystery of God, the gospel, would end when this angel sounded which was begun in 1840.

Elder W.W. Stebbins said that the primary point to be remembered is that it was in the power of this people to delay or hasten the day, and that as were all anxious to see that day, we should all seek the proper preparation to meet it.

Elder Hyatt admitted that from some standpoints the coming of the Lord might appear a long way off as so many thousands have not yet been warned. If we did not believe that God's hand is controlling we might well think that we would not live to see the end. But I feel that we shall see the day when God's people will rise with mighty power and hasten the work.

Elder Shireman gave a description of the views of a prominent editor ridiculing the idea of passing religious enactments, but a few weeks ago the gentleman wrote a letter admitting his change of views and probability that the Fifty-first Congress would pass such bills, and so the nearness of the end be apparent. I believe the people of God are preparing for the battle and the end must be very near.

Attention was also called to the means at the command of the parties at work for religious legislation to work up rapidly, a public sentiment in their favor. Allusion was made to the influence of Miss Willard, president of the W.C.T.U., over audiences and individuals; the combination of this organization, the Sabbath Union Sunday school, forming a wonderfully effective power for this work, influencing the unthinking masses and working up public sentiment.

Elder Sarnont called attention to the papacy or the mystery of iniquity, the people not then understanding the movement, and that the work in our country is the image to it, the power behind each, as Paul tells us being Satan himself, who works in darkness, deceptively.

Elder States asked for information in reference to the Turk planting his tabernacle between the mountains and said some claimed it meant the removal of the papacy to this country, but Elder Ferrin showed from Revelations 16, this could not be because the great battle was to be fought at Jerusalem, to be followed soon after by the coming of the Lord.

Elder D.T. Jones called attention to Daniel 11:45, that in the kingdoms brought to view in the latter verses, Rome was not mentioned after the 45th, verse, and our government not at all, so that the movement could not be the papacy, but does refer to the power spoken of in the 45th verse.

Elder Smith Sharp called attention to the fact that when the Turk retreats, Christ comes, but the papacy was to be destroyed by the brightness of His coming.

Elder Stebbins said the miracle-working power was connected with the United States which was not true of the Turkish power, spiritualism having its rise in this country.

It must be understood that the argument of Elder Sharp does not represent so much what he really believes as it does positions tending to draw out questions and discussion which was the object aimed at.

THE AFTERNOON SERMON

MRS. WHITE BEING UNABLE TO SPEAK, Elder A.T. Jones continued his sermons on "church government."

"Beginning at 1 Corinthians 14:11–25, when it is shown that the church at Corinth seemed to more earnestly desire the gift of tongues than any other; so Paul tells them rather to desire prophecy, because an unknown tongue was a sign to unbelievers, while prophesying was for edification of the church, speaking in tongues being of no profit to the hearers unless interpreted. Now read verses 26 and onward. Here we have the direction to keep silent if one has the gift of tongues and there be no interpreter. Then what is the use of the gift if it requires the two to make the gift available? Why not let the interpreter tell it at once? Because, verse 22, it is for a sign to unbelievers. Now, if all spoke with tongues the unbelievers would think all were lunatics, but if one prophesy his inmost secrets may be revealed and he be convicted and repent. For an unbeliever to hear his neighbor whom he knows get up and talk in an unknown tongue, and another of his neighbors arise and explain his words, he is forced to realize there is some high power exercising all. This I introduce to show you how the gifts work together. Now, verses 27, 28 and onward–ye are members of the body and

God has set them in the body as He pleases, illustrating the church and its members under the figure of the body, and has set the members not to please them, but to please Himself. Therefore if you and I try to set the members in the church as it suits us, will it be likely to do good work as it would if we let God do it? If all are controlled by the Lord will my actions please Him if I take out of His hands the control of the members? How has God set the members: apostles, prophets, teachers, after that miracles, helps, governments, diversity of tongues. The gift of teaching then is not to be counted as one of the least, standing third in the list and before miracles, so then it is a greater thing to instruct others in the word of God than it is to work miracles.

"Now turn to Romans 12:6–8 and read of other gifts that are compliments to each other. One may have the faculty of teaching, yet he may not be able to exhort, which another does possess without the ability to teach. They working together are a help to one another. God could and would bless each separately, but united they would become a power. That being so, then there never ought to be room in the church of Christ for jealousy or envy. Paul carries these things further, 1 Corinthians 12:31. But he says 'covet earnestly the best gifts.' Is not that then a commandment of the Lord? Are we doing it? If not, why not? Read also 14:1, desire spiritual gifts; also chapter 12:1, who would not leave you ignorant—Christ. Are we ignorant? Do we study spiritual gifts? If we do not believe in them we shall be ignorant of them, because faith must always go before knowledge. If we believe, desire follows, and what next: 'covet earnestly the best gifts. Yet show I you a more excellent way.'

"Suppose we could get all these gifts by desiring them, what good would it do us? None whatever. If a company in this place could speak with the tongues of angels and had all the other gifts, and had all benevolence and faith, they would be worthless. If then we could obtain all these gifts simply by coveting them, they would be profitless without the love of God in the heart shed abroad by faith in Jesus Christ; we would be a tinkling cymbal. How then do we obtain them that they may be a benefit to us? By getting the love of God. If given to us because we want them simply, we would not appreciate them and use them to the honor and glory of God. What then is charity and what does it do? 'Charity suffereth long and is kind.' Will suffer and be kind while it continues, will not rebel or lose temper. If we are wrongly accused ought we to be glad that it is not true, and thank God that it is not? 1 Peter 2:19–23. It is no glory if we be corrected for our faults and submit, but if we exercise patience under wrong reproach then God is pleased with us, that is acceptable with God. That is the grace of God, which enables us to bear it. One who is in the right can afford to wait, and will never lose by doing it. Christ is an example of this to us. The man who knows he is right and innocent, can commit his cause to the Lord and wait patiently, He will never vindicate him, and in just the right way. That was

Christ's method and He was the embodiment of charity. Charity envieth not. Envy means to see against, to look askance at pain, uneasiness or discontent excited by another's superiority or success, accompanied generally with a desire to see him unsuccessful. So then whoever envies another confesses his own unworthiness. Have we had such feelings? Very well, that is envy and not charity.

THE EVENING LECTURE...

BY A. T. JONES

"IN CONTINUING THIS PART OF MY SUBJECT, I want to show further that Constantine was a Christian only from political motives and a pagan always from convictions. He read from Milman's Christianity to show that up to the time of his acceptance of the head of the church he was outwardly pagan, that the statues erected by him to Apollo show him to have his favorite god. In 312 he claims to have seen a vision of the cross, and he erected a holy standard in honor of this vision and Christ. You remember I told you about the dreaming of Maxeutius and its comparison to the dreaming of Pharaoh. It was at this time Constantine assumed the garb of a Christian. But, as Milman says, it was 'the Christianity of the warrior,' and he said his barbarities showed the same pagan hearts as before. In the labarum he erected the blended symbols of both Christianity and the images of himself and family; because the image of the emperor was always worshiped by the Romans, so that both Christians and pagans could worship at it.

"One of his titles was Penitix Maximus. The superstition of his youth, says Miliman in substance, clung to him, and speaking of the prophecy pillar, the head of Constantine was substituted for that of Apollo, and then asks, 'is this paganism approximating to Christianity or Christianity degenerating to paganism?' Dr. Schaff says Constantine adopted Christianity as a superstition. In fact, the bishops were afraid to compel him to be baptized for fear he would renounce Christianity and turn pagan again, and become a very jealous of a pagan philosopher, Sapates, who was a friend of Constantine, fearing he would turn pagan under his influence, so trumped up a charge against him and he was hastily executed. After his death no one could tell if he had been a Christian. Milman says that he did not want to alienate his heathen friend, while the Christians did not dare to proceed too far in their efforts to force him to excel his authority in abolishing paganism, so that all the time paganism was openly professed and was the religion of the empire confronting Christianity, so that after his death both religions vied for Constantine. He was deified by the pagans and worshipped by the Christians. Stanley, in his *History of the Christian Church*, says: 'So passed away the first Christian emperor, the first defender of the faith the first imperial patron of the Papal See, and of the whole eastern church the founder of the holy place pagan and Christian, orthodox and heretical, liberal and fanatical, not to be initiated or admired, but much to be remembered, and deeply to be studied.'

"Now these are some of the authentic records of history, so you can judge to some extent what kind of man Constantine was.

"Now the Sunday legislation of Constantine. Reading from Neander, quoting from Sozomen, read the second of the first Sunday law to show it was in behalf of both pagans and Christians. This is the law that was not preserved, only the second remaining. This one embodied Friday as well as Sunday. The date of this law is unknown. The purpose was that the day might be devoted to devotion. Now remember that the Romans had festival days, but no day set apart for worship. So it is not correct to say that Sunday was a day of worship among the pagans. That is a papal idea, solely setting it apart for worship, separate from the other days. This is why Constantine called it the venerable day of the sun, because he did not dare to offend the pagans. The Christians then were worshipping the sun. The church would first receive a person as a catechumen, and these would turn first to the west, the realm of Satan, and then turn to the east to worship 'the sun of Righteousness,' changing the pagan worship of the sun to the sun of righteousness. The law of 321 you are familiar with, compelling town people to rest on Sunday. Milman says the rescript for the religious observance of Sunday, 'which enjoined the suspension of all public business and private labor ... was enacted for the whole Roman empire, yet unless we had direct proof that the decree set forth the Christian reason for the sanctity of the day, it may be doubted whether the act would not be received by the greater part of the empire as merely adding one more festival to the Fasti of the empire.'

"Have we this direct proof? No. I read what Milman says: 'The rescript commanding the celebration of the Christian Sabbath, bears no allusion to its peculiar sanctity as a Christian institution.' When this Sunday law was made it embraced the whole Roman world, and Constantine had a prayer written that both Christians and pagans could apply to the God they worshipped, and the soldiers were drawn up in line and forced to repeat it in unison. This law was given solely to please the bishops who had transferred the sanctity of God's Sabbath to the counterfeit of their theocracy, prevailing upon the emperor to enforce their desired observance of it, so the day as a day of worship is papal entirely. Milman calls this 'the new paganism,' because pagans could acquiesce without scruple in its observance. Now all this shows that Sunday has no civil basis. It was religious in every particular. Did God ordain it? No. Did Caesar ordain it? No. It sprang from the church, having its basis in paganism, so then it is never to be rendered to God, to the state, or to anyone in heaven or earth. The bishops had to have this institution to complete their theocracy and to compel the people to act in conformity with their idea, now there were people living then that knew this was in opposition to all known rights, and the bishops knew it too."

The speaker read again from Alexander to show that the custom in the church was established by a single law that all Christians should abstain from labor on Sunday, but it was made more effective by the use of the power of the state, through the making of the Sunday law. The same twenty-ninth canon that established this custom is the same one who cursed anyone for keeping the Sabbath of the Lord. Can there be any better fulfillment of the prophecy that says, 'He shall think to change times and laws?' There is where the papacy made their effort to change the law of God.

"Now for some of the reasons the bishops gave for obtaining these Sunday laws. Of course all the men compelled to be idle drifted into the circuses and theaters, and such vast crowds would attend that large numbers of men had to be employed, and so Christians were hired, so the bishops argued that the people going to such places made it necessary for the circuses and theaters to employ extra hands and so compel Christians to work 'against their will,' so Manden says that in 326 all kinds of labor was prohibited, and so on festival days the circuses and theaters greatly interfered with the worship of the church, and argued that the people would be worshippers if it was not for the greater attraction of the shows, so they asked for laws that would compel them to observe the Sunday. Now the very arguments used then are now being used, almost word for word, and if we have access to the Vatican library the similarity would, no doubt, be more apparent. The bishops claimed then that the circuses and theaters were persecuting Christians by compelling them to work on Sunday, and they called it persecution. The very same thing is said now of the railroads, etc. Now having compelled men to be idle, that they might be devoted, they were compelled to take away their amusement to force them to be devoted, so will it be now. Not only that but they must put devotion in the place of amusement to keep them from hell and start them heavenward, and having started in this path that last must come, the inquisition to reach the heart to save them from ruin. Never forget the inquisition was never a punishment for wickedness but to save souls from hell. They did not torment a man because he was wicked but to get him to confess for that would bring pardon and to ensure his safety; they would then kill him while holy, that he could not have a chance to sin again. Then is not the inquisition the very theory of the Sunday observance? Now, I do not say that the inquisition in this country will be the same as in Rome, but the same practice will bring the same result here as in Rome, and the third angel's message says that death will be decreed against all who will not observe Sunday in opposition to the Sabbath. Now all who advocate Sunday laws do not see all this, or do all expect a theocracy, but all their arguments are theocratical ones, and lead to all the results I have enumerated. Many would be horrified if they thought their action would lead to this, but they will be led along step by step until they do not see the end just as it must come.

"Now another thing. The canon of Laodicea cursed those who kept the Sabbath. Why was this necessary? Because there were people keeping the Sabbath, and they were warning the people against the fraud—so the bishops were compelled to stop belittling the Sunday. Now, who do the national reformers say are the real opposers of the Sunday observance? Is it not the Seventh-day Adventists? This they admit, and say it is the hardest of all to meet, because the opposition comes from the Bible record. When the statement was once made that Adventists not only wanted to keep the seventh day but tried to break down the observance of Sunday and the question was asked what should be done, the reply was, 'They must not be allowed to take such a course.' That is what they expect to do to us. God has given the message to us and the course we must take is to try to destroy all respect for the Sunday, because it is a day for which no man should have any respect."

THE CAMP MEETING

Much Rain And Mud,
But An Increase Of Visitors

Great Interest in the Exercises—A Large Attendance at the Sabbath Schools—Instructed by Mrs. Haskell, of Denver, and Elder W.H. Wakeham—Able Sermons **and** Lectures.

Special Correspondence of the CAPITAL

FOREST PARK, OTTAWA, KAN., MAY 12…

SATURDAY, THE SEVENTH DAY, THE BIBLE SABBATH, began Friday evening at sundown, so that the people all assembled for prayer at that time, and early again Saturday morning, when the young people met in a separate tent, which is the beginning of a series of like meetings to continue through the camp meeting.

At 8:45 came the principle event of the day, the Sabbath School, in which, in four divisions, the senior, intermediate, primary and kindergarten, 41 classes were formed with a membership of 253. The classes were distributed in the large tabernacle according to the program already published in the CAPITAL, and the kindergarten children formed a pleasing sight up on the rostrum surrounding their tables seated in the diminutive chairs of this department. Mrs. C.P. Haskell, of Denver, reviewed the little ones on the lesson "Life of Enoch," and Elder W.H. Wakeham the senior division on "Unbelief and Punishment."

THE SABBATH MORNING SERMON…

BY A.T. JONES

"MATTHEW 6:33—'SEEK YE FIRST THE KINGDOM OF GOD and His righteousness,' is the subject today. We notice first whose righteousness we are to seek. It is God's. We must seek and find it, or we will not be saved. Nothing else will avail. We must know, however, where to seek for it and how, because we often seek for it in the wrong places; for instance, as many do, in the law of God, and through keeping it. We will never find it there. This is not the place to seek for it. This is not saying that the righteousness of God is not there. The commandments are the righteousness of God, but we will never find it there. In Romans 2:17–18 we see that the law is clearly pointed out, through which, if we are instructed, we are called of God. Then they, being the will of God, it would be impossible for the Lord himself to be better than the Ten Commandments require us to be. The Lord's will must be the expression of what He is Himself; hence it is impossible He should be better than His law. To keep His commandments, then, means that we shall be as good as God is, so we read in 1 John 3:7: 'He that doeth righteousness, is righteous even as he is righteous.' Now see Deuteronomy 6:25; Isaiah 51:7—the people who do the law of God are righteous, even as God is righteous, then to keep them means that man must be like God in character. Then the righteousness of God is in His law, but it is not revealed to men by the law, Romans 1:16–17, the righteousness of God is revealed in the gospel to men, and not in the law. It is in the law, but it is not revealed there to us because we are sinners, and sin has so darkened our mind that we cannot see it there, and therefore our vision has to be enlightened by some other means, which is the gospel, where we must seek for it, Romans 3:21. The righteousness of God is made known without the law. How? By faith in Jesus Christ, through the gospel, and not by the law.

"Now read again Romans 1:16–17 and this will be clear. To show this further, Romans 10:4. Christ is the end of the law for righteousness to everyone that believeth. Does not this say the same as the others? We have lost often the real point in this text to use it against those who claim the commandments are abolished, who claim Christ ended the law, and we claiming it means 'the purpose of' the law, but the point in this text is that Christ is the purpose of the law 'for righteousness' to us as we cannot get it by the law, Romans 8:3. The law was ordained to life, righteousness, holiness, justification, but because of sin it can not be this to us, so what it cannot do Christ does for us. Then, if we seek it in the wrong place we lose the righteousness of Christ.

"Now righteousness must come from the same source as does life; they are inseparable. Romans 8:3, Paul uses the terms here interchangeably, so also Galatians 3:21, showing that righteousness must come to us from the same source as life, and that is, Christ. Romans 6:23, this we have also preached, but he said before that the wages of sin is death but the gift of God is eternal life, and so we have always claimed eternal life to be a gift, but we have not claimed the same righteousness as being a gift through Jesus Christ. Why was it necessary that something was given, to have life? Because the wages of sin was death. If a law could give life, it would be by the law. If the law was a secondary form and God could have made another, and better, it would not suffice because if men could not keep an inferior law they could not keep a superior, consequently no law could give the life.

"Therefore Christ came to be the purpose of the law to everyone that believeth. Now we want to see what righteousness there is in the law for us, and will become convinced it is our own, which is the very best we can ever get out of the law. If I take the highest and most comprehensive view of the law I can, and live up to it, is that a satisfying of the law? No, because it is not a high enough view of it, because the mind is all darkened by sin, and man's comprehension is not broad enough to grasp the height and breadth of it, and so it does not meet the requirements of the law. It is our own righteousness then, and not God's we see in the law and we see ourselves (the extent of our vision) and not the face of God. Often we think we do right and afterwards see it was not so. If it was God's righteousness at that time, God would be imperfect. It is only in Christ that we can ever see the righteousness of God. But God is the gospel and the gospel is Christ, and so by the law can no man be accounted righteous. We must then have something more than the law to enable us to understand God's righteousness and to comprehend the law. That something 'is Christ Jesus, in who is the fullness of the Godhead bodily.'

"I read now Romans 10:1–3; here we have a people seeking earnestly for righteousness. Whose? Their own. Did they find it? No, Romans 9:31–33, being ignorant of Christ's righteousness. They would not believe Christ or Paul, but sought it by the works of the law. Now read verse 30; the Gentiles found it having faith, and not being satisfied with their own righteousness, as did the Pharisees who trusted in themselves that they were righteous. This, too, is where the law will bring us if we try to obtain righteousness through it, but when, having faith in Christ, a man sees his sins and longs for the righteousness of God. Knowing that it is the goodness, purity and righteousness of Christ that makes him so, he will become righteous.

"Philippians 3:4–9; here was a Pharisee who lived up to the broadest view of the law of God, he could obtain and was blameless, yet he gave it all up for Christ. Galatians 2:21, if 'righteousness comes by the law then Christ is dead in vain,' our own righteousness is all, then, we can get out of the law, and that the righteousness of God can come only by Jesus Christ. What is our own righteousness? Isaiah 64:6. Our righteousness is as filthy rags. We have all sinned and come short of the glory of God. What is sin? When Israel came out of Egypt, they knew not God, remembering only that Abraham, Isaac, and Jacob had a God, but knew nothing more to make them understand their condition and what sin was He took one of their own words and applied it to his purpose. He took a word meaning 'missed its mark' and used it to express sin. Now we have all sinned and come short—that is what Paul means—we have 'missed the mark." Then the more righteousness of the law a man has the worse he is off, the more ragged is he. Now turn to

Zechariah 3:1–8. Mrs. White declares this chapter to be a prophecy of this present time. Here we have Joshua standing clothed in his own righteousness and Christ takes it off and clothes him with the righteousness of God. Now Joshua had been doing the best he could, but would he have been saved? No. How often we hear people say 'I do the best I can,' and believe they will be saved. Joshua was reclothed and was to stand with the angels. If then our righteousness is all taken away and Christ clothes us with God's righteousness, then to walk in His law, we will stand with the angels. So then read Isaiah 54:17, last part. Christ, in all His references in the New Testament, repeats only what God had already spoken. Now, Isaiah 61:10, that is the song we are to sing, therefore righteousness is the gift of God as surely as is life, and if we try to get it in any other way we shall fail. In Romans 5:12–18, we read that as sin came by one, the righteousness of one brought the free gift of life upon man. So also Romans 3:21–26; it was to declare God's righteousness that Christ came. Now taking Romans 5:13–17 we find here a free gift and notice, particularly verse 17. Righteousness is the gift of life to every one who believeth, and Jesus Christ will ever be the purpose of the law to every one who believeth. It is Christ's obedience that avails and not ours that beings righteousness to us. Well, then let us stop trying to do the will of God in our own strength. Stop it all. Put it away from you forever. Let Christ's obedience do it all for you and gain the strength to pull the bow so that you can hit the mark.

"Why did the Savior come as an infant instead of a man? To die on the cross would have met the penalty. Because He loved a child and met all the temptations a child meets and never sinned—so that any child can stand in His place and resist in His strength; and He lived also as a youth, a man full grown, weaving for us a robe of righteousness to cover us (not cover our filthy garments, as that would be a mixture), taking the filthy garments away and put His own in their place, so that all may have it if they will. Now if righteousness is the gift of God, and comes by the gospel, then what is the use of the law? There are several, but they may be used wrongfully. The law entered that the offense might abound, Romans 3:19, 5:17—the law speaks to sinners that all may become guilty before God to show people their guilt. Now verse 20, the law is to reveal sin to us—unrighteousness, not righteousness—Christ reveals the latter, the law the former. The law of God cannot allow a single sin in any degree whatever. If it did, and condoned even a single thought that was not perfect, it would sink a soul into perdition. The law is perfect. If it accepts imperfection the Lord must accept it and admit that He is imperfect, because the law is the representation of His character. In the fact that the law demands perfection lies the hope of all mankind, because if it could overlook a sin to a single degree, no one could ever be free from sin, as the law would never make that sin known, and it could never be forgiven by which alone man can be saved. The day is coming when the law will have revealed the last sin and we will stand perfect before Him and be saved with an eternal salvation. The perfection of the law of God is that it will show us all our sins, and then a perfect Saviour stands ready to take them all away. When God makes known all our sins it is not to condemn us, but to save us, so it is a token of His love for us, therefore, whenever a sin is made known to you, it is a token of God's love for you, because the Saviour stands ready to take it away. That is why God has given us a Saviour and the gospel. He wants us all to believe in Him, come to Him and be loved.

"Read Matthew 5:6. Are there not many here who hunger and thirst for righteousness? Do you want to be filled? Look not then at the law, but the cross of Christ. Read Ephesians 3:14–19, rooted and grounded in faith through His love in our heart. Colossians 2:9–10, for we will be complete in Christ. There is completeness, joy, peace, goodness, righteousness forever."

ELDER A.T. JONES' EVENING LECTURE

"THE SUBJECT TONIGHT IS 'THE EVILS OF A UNION OF CHURCH and State.' I quote from Draper's *Intellectual Development of Europe*. 'It was the aim of Constantine to make theology a branch of politics, it was the hope of every bishop in the empire to make politics a branch of theology.' Another quotation is this, these being the two ideas upon which the old and the coming theocracy is and will be built. 'When once a political aspirant has bidden with the multitude for power and still depends on their pleasure for effective support it is no easy thing to refuse their wishes or hold back from their demands.' Thus Constantine had virtually sold himself to this power that he wished to control and could never ignore it and hold his position. Schaff in his *Church History* gives this estimate of Constantine: 'He was distinguished by that genuine political wisdom which, putting itself at the head of the age, clearly saw that idolatry had outlived itself in the Roman empire, and that Christianity alone could breathe new vigor into it and furnish it moral support.

"It was then entirely as a political thing that he embraced Christianity. 'Now Constantine adopted Christianity first by a superstition and put it by the side of his heathen superstition till finally in his conviction the Christian vanquished the pagan though without itself developing into a pure and enlightened faith.' Here you have the history of Constantine in a few words. Did Constantine establish Christianity as the Roman religion? Schaff says: 'He presumed to preach the gospel, he called himself the bishop of bishops, he convened the first general council and made Christianity the religion of the empire long before his baptism.' But he did not issue an edict making it the state religion.

"A statement from Hilman, which he calls the legal establishment of Christianity: 'Christianity may now be said to have ascended the imperial throne; with the single exception of Julian, from this period the monarch of the Roman empire professed the religion of the gospel.' I want to notice tonight what Constantine did for the church and what befell it as soon as politics became incorporated with it and the effect it had upon the church, state, and society, and what it will do again. Neander says: 'With the commencement of this period the church entered into an entirely different relation to the state. It did not merely become a whole, recognized or legal, and tolerated by the state, but the state itself declared its principles to be those to which everything must be subordinated.'

"This is the same argument that the reformers use now that they will remain distinct revolving round one another, but you will see the impossibility of this 'church and state constituted, henceforth, two wholes, one interpenetrating the other, and standing in relation of mutual action and reaction. The advantageous influence of this was, that the church would now exert its transforming power also on the relations of the state; but the measure and character of this power depended on the state of the inner life in the church itself. It was now necessary that one of two things should happen: either the spirit of Christianity, as it became more widely diffused, must—not by a sudden and glaring revolution, but by its power in the heart, which is far mightier than any arm of flesh—gradually introduce the order of law, in the place of arbitrary despotism; or the corruption of the state would introduce itself into the church, as it actually did in the Byzantine empire.' Which did happen, why the later and this must inevitably happen because a pure church will never ask for civil power, so long as she has the power of God, but losing this she will grasp for anything she can get. 'Furthermore the church was now exposed to the temptations of appropriating a foreign might for the prosecutions of its ends.' Mark now this statement: 'A temptation ever ready to assail man, the moment the spirit is no longer sovereign alone.' This is a piece of philosophy you should ever remember, and is true in ecclesiastical affairs as well as civil enforcement of discipline. Now as to what Constantine did for the church the speaker read many extracts to show how the Christians, living as they pleased, would will their property to the church, and that act carried them through to heaven. By this means the church became immensely wealthy. In 313 Constantine freed the clergy from all state taxation, the removal of a great burden. The result was hundreds joined the clergy to get rid of these burdens. These two corrupting influences soon made the bishops almost equal in power to the emperor, himself, and opened the way for men to profess Christianity for power and wealth.

"Next Constantine would build a church where there was not a Christian, and sending a bishop and clergy there would pay a piece of gold and a white garment to whoever would be baptized and support every convert. The result was crowds would become Christians. In places where the Christians were few he would offer special inducements, and whole cities would turn to Christianity. Pagans, philosophers and teachers would turn Christian to teach paganism in the schools. Just as soon as Christianity had political influence and political favor to bestow it brought the very worst characters in the church, and so it will be in every church where politics is given a prominent place, and the outcome can only be a papacy. If any nation favors any particular religion men will flock to it for the emoluments to be obtained. The baser element will push itself to the front and use their positions for political advancement. Neander says, 'The more the church strove after outward dominion, the more she was liable to go astray, and to forget in this outward power, her own intrinsic essence as a church of the spirit, and the more easy it became for outward power to have dominion over her.'

" 'By the temporal advantages connected with the spiritual profession (they called a man to office not so much for his spiritual qualifications as for his political power) many who had neither the inward call nor any other qualifications for this order were led to aspire after church offices; so that in fact numbers became Christians solely with a view of obtaining some post in the church and enjoying the emoluments therewith connected.' When that man ran for a bishopric, and these men supported him, he had to do as they wished and preach such doctrine as pleased them or he was removed. 'Men were made bishops who were not Christians.' What would now be called a worldling. This being called a Christian nation, all will have a voice in the church, and the officers will deal in political intrigue for office and the rabble will force their candidates upon the church, and as in Rome the worst kind of men will be elected to keep them from harming the church. 'It sometimes happened that by the voice of the whole community, or of a powerful party in it, some individual standing high in their confidence was proclaimed bishop. But as, in the then existing state of the church, the most pious and they who had a right conception of the essence of the spiritual office, and who had at heart the spiritual interests of the community, did not constitute the majority and the most powerful party.'

" 'Thus, in the year 361, the popular party at Caesarea in Cappadocia, supported by the garrison of the place, insisted upon having for their bishop one of the civil magistrates, Eusebius, who had not, as yet, been baptized, and the provincial bishops, many of whom perhaps had a better man in mind, allowed themselves to be forced to ordain him.' Now Schaff tells more about that than Neander: 'Sometimes the people acted under outside considerations, and the management of demagogues, and demanded unworthy or ignorant men for the highest offices, working up the primaries as is done now in large cities like Chicago, New York, and etc.' In a note he says: 'Many were elected on account of their badness, to prevent the mischief they would otherwise do.' Do you not see how this corrupting influence drew the church down and down in degradation. Another statement from Neander: 'The vast numbers who, from external considerations, without any inward call, joined themselves to the Christian communities, served to introduce into the Christian church all the corruptions of the heathen world. Pagan vices, pagan delusion, pagan superstitions, took the garb and name of Christianity, and were thus enabled to exert a more corrupting influence on the Christian life. Such were those who, without any real interest whatever in the concerns of religion, living half in paganism and half in an outward show of Christianity, composed the crowds that thronged the churches on the festivals of the Christians, and the theatres on the festivals of the pagans. That is the papacy, and what then is the papacy but, paganism under a Christian name.

" 'It was natural that the bad element which had outwardly assumed the Christian garb, should push itself more prominently to notice in public life. Hence it was more sure to attract the common gaze, while the genuine Christian temper loved retirement, and created less sensation.'

"The genuine Christians were pushed into the background. From the day Constantine proposed Christianity, the history of the church has not been the history of Christianity. The history of Christianity closed with the acts of the apostles, to be opened again when Luther left the church, the balance is the history of the papacy. So then the worldly Christians were as separated from the genuine Christians as the pagan had been. In Milman I read: 'On the incorporation of the church with the state, the coordinate civil and religious magistracy maintained each its separate powers. On the one side, as far as the actual celebration of the ecclesiastical ceremonial, and in their own internal affairs in general; on the other, in the administration of the military, judicial, and fiscal affairs of the state, the bounds of their respective authority were clear and distinct.' The assertion then that the church and state constitute two wholes is not possible. There are a few things where the jurisdiction of each is clearly defined, but there are thousands of points where it would be impossible to tell where the jurisdiction of the church stops and that of the state begins. 'So far the theory was distinct and perfect; each had his separate and exclusive sphere, yet there could not but appear a debatable ground on which the two authorities came into collision, and neither could altogether refrain from invading the territory of his ally or antagonist.

"When you get religion into politics where is the limit going to stop? The church takes cognizance of every relation of life; now then, if she has control of the civil power, how can you prevent her carrying it into the thoughts of the heart? It cannot be done. The best things when perverted become the worst. So of Christianity, it being the best thing the world ever saw, perverted will be the worst. On the other hand, the state was supreme over all its subjects, even over the clergy in their character of citizens. But there was another prolific source of difference. The clergy in one sense, from being the representative body, had begun to consider themselves the church; but in another and more legitimate sense, the state, when Christian, as comprehending all the Christians of the empire, became the church. Which was the legislative body? The whole community of Christians or the Christian aristocracy, who were in one sense the admitted rulers?

69

"By this time they had made the distinction of the 'laity' and the 'clergy' which did not belong to the church of Christ, who then chose the officers. Did not the state fairly succeed to all the rights of the laity, more particularly when privileges and endowments attached to the ecclesiastical offices were conferred or guaranteed by the state, and therefore might appear in justice revocable, or liable to be regulated by the civil power? Don't you see that every step in the papacy is logical, and do you not see that in the work of the reformers each of these steps is in it, and must logically follow. 'When once the civil power was recognized as cognizant of ecclesiastical offenses, where was that power to end?' Of the religious condition of Rome at the time, Milman says: 'Thus in a great degree while the Roman world became Christian in outward worship and in faith, it remained heathen, or even at some periods worse than heathenism, in its better times, as to beneficence, gentleness, purity, social virtue, humanity and peace. Heresy of opinions became almost the only crime against which excommunication pointed its thunders. Thus, Christianity became at the same time more peremptory dogmatic, and less influential; it assumed the supreme dominion over the mind, while it held but an imperfect and partial control over the passions and appetites. The theology of the gospel was the religion of the world; the spirit of the gospel very far from the ruling influence of mankind. Whenever a national religion is established, heresy is the highest crime, because the state becomes the guardian of the soul, and expects to be held responsible for its guardianship; hence punishes blasphemy against the established religion as speaking against the soul itself. That is the kind of system that comes in whenever you have a union of church and state'"

THE SERMON ON RIGHTEOUSNESS...

BY A.T. JONES

"THE SUBJECT IS HOW TO OBTAIN THAT RIGHTEOUSNESS of which we read yesterday, the righteousness of God which only will avail. Romans 3:24, justified means accounted righteous. How? Freely. By what means? Grace. What is grace? Favor. Let us ever believe this text, holding fast to it forever. In regard to grace we read Romans 11:6, which means we are justified freely by His grace without works, otherwise it is not grace. Another reference, Ephesians 2:5 8–9,; now turn to Romans 4:4 with Romans 10:4. You see then why, if it be of works it is no more of grace. If we have to work to obtain grace, then we bring the Lord in debt to us, and if He does not pay He does us injustice. To pay is not a favor, it is paying a debt. We are accounted righteous freely by His grace and that not of works. I read now Romans 4:1–2. Abraham was the father of all them that believe—the spiritual father—can we expect to receive more than He did? If he was justified by works, He gloried in Himself. Now put Romans 4:2 with 1 Corinthians 1:27–31. The Lord has arranged it that all should glorify him and not themselves, because to glorify a sinner, a rebel, would not be proper for a government, allowing them to come back in harmony with it, glorifying themselves. All the woe in the world came through Satan attempting to glorify himself. 'I will be like the Most High.' To allow a sinner then to glorify himself would force pardon being extended to Satan, also. Now, Christ is made unto us righteousness and sanctification, and we glory in Christ and not ourselves. If we believe on Him our faith is counted to us for righteousness. But can the Lord justify the ungodly? Yes, Christ came to justify sinners, so read carefully this verse, Romans 4:5. The first thing then to learn is that we are ungodly and confess it, God will count him righteous. The Lord cannot justify and save any who cannot see their true condition. There is joy in heaven over one sinner that repenteth, more than over ninety and nine that need no repentance. The Saviour came not to call righteous but sinners to repentance, then none but sinners will be saved. Now Romans 4:16, 'therefore it is of faith.' Why? That it might be by grace, 'to the end that it may be saved.'

"Faith is the easiest and most natural thing in the world. There is nothing wonderful about faith, as some think, and say 'I try to believe and if I can't then how can I?' But we can believe God with the same faculties we believe others. Don't try to believe—quit it—and believe. We either believe or don't believe—then why not believe? Believe as a child, don't reason it out. Faith goes in advance of reason, knowledge and all else. At school the teacher pointed out a letter and told us 'That is A,' and that is all the evidence we have of it. We believed it, now let us receive the kingdom of heaven as we did when a child the words of your teacher. If we reason on faith we can never believe, because to reason faith is unreasonable because the effort of reason always produces doubt. It begins and ends with a 'how.' Because faith is the simplest and easiest thing for all, God put His salvation in the surest place, that we might have it and know that He has it. Now, Romans 5:6, 8, 10, Christ died for you because you are ungodly, and He died for the ungodly, and you can be counted righteous right now if you will believe it. Christ's death reconciled the world unto God but it never saved any or ever can. His death met the penalty of the law, but we are saved by Christ's life. Read Romans 4:25. By His death then we have reconciliation, by His life justification, and by His second coming we have salvation—all these being necessary to complete the plan of salvation. The law of God shows a man to be ungodly—and as by the law is the knowledge of sin, which is ungodliness—we will call it now sin, so turn to Proverbs 28:13, mercy being treating one better than he deserves. Remember, believe this fully; our habit has been to confess our sins and then doubt the forgiveness and carry them all away with us, obtaining no peace because we doubted. 'God never appointed us to wrath.' 1 Thessalonians 5:9. He shows them laws to save us from them, the knowledge of them being a token of His love, that there is Jesus to take them all from us. He calls us to obtain salvation. So do not take the knowledge of your sins as a token of His wrath. Whosoever confesses his sins shall be saved, Romans 4:6–7.

"Now 1 John 1:9, 'If we confess our sins He will forgive and cleanse us from all our sins.' Believe this fully and go free. How many go to the soul confessing and never believe they are forgiven? To believe part of the word and not all is infidelity. 'Man shall live by every word that proceedeth out of the mouth of the Lord.' To confess a sin and not believe in its forgiveness is infidelity. Don't wait for feeling—that has nothing to do with faith. How can anyone know how he ought to feel when sins are forgiven? If you trust to feeling you are like a wave of the sea tossed by the winds to and fro. Often revivalists tell mourners how he felt when he was forgiven, and they try to feel as he did and fail, as no two can ever feel just alike and so no one can tell if converted. Faith does not rest on evidence. If it rests on the reasonableness of a thing, it rests on reason and not faith. If it rests on the confidence we have in the person, and that person contradicts himself, then where is faith? If one says, 'I will do some great thing,' and I believe him; if he comes again and says something that uproots all he previously said, what am I to do? Now let me prove this: Abraham was justified by faith and it was counted to him for righteousness. Read the account of it, Genesis 15:5 and onward. Sometime after that Isaac was born, and growing up, Abraham was told to offer him up, directly against the promise. Where did his faith come in? By believing the promise independent of appearances. That was faith furnishing its own evidence.. Abraham believed it until all came right because God had promised it would. Now turn to Romans 4:16–22; Abraham against hope believed in hope, his faith furnishing the hope, confidence and evidence. Never let our feelings, then, have any control over our faith. Feelings belong to Satan. Relegate them to him. 'The just shall live by faith.' Brethren, let us live that way. When we believe, it puts Christ in place of the sin, and when Satan comes to attack us he finds only Christ, and then we have the victory over Satan, not delivering us from temptation, but giving us power to conquer temptation, and gaining the victory, that particular temptation never comes again. We are conquerors there forever. If you want feeling about this, praise the Lord because He ever pardons your sin and because you believe His promise, and there will be feeling enough within you to be satisfactory. Look for God, and He will put a song in your mouth.

"Now, do you believe my opening text, that we are justified freely? Often we sin and feel so ashamed and bad over it we wait a few days to get a little better before we go to the Lord for forgiveness. We try to make ourselves good first. There is a tendency in every soul to this. That is justification by works, the same as fasting or punishing oneself first. This is the root of monkery and all the penances in the Catholic Church. Then, if we do not want to be papist, let us quit. We have done no better, but the sin has lost the honor before us, and we are better in our own eyes, and then confess only our surface sin, so the Holy Spirit shows us again the sin that was covered up. Now the—only way to get rid of it is to confess it at once, because the

Lord shows us a sin just as it is, and right then, so that He can forgive it fully and completely. When we try to patch up our sin by doing better, we are putting on more and more of the filthy rags spoken of by Isaiah, which is our own righteousness. Let us read Revelation 3:14–18. Let us trust the Lord and believe His promise.

THE CAMP MEETING

Mrs. E.G. White Speaks Before
A Large Concourse Of People

Arrival of Elder O.A. Olsen From England, President of the General
Conference—Large Audiences Present Since the Rain—Five Sermons
and Lectures—Interest Increasing.

Special correspondence of the CAPITAL

CAMP MEETING GROUND, OTTAWA, KAN., May 14...

NOW THAT THE SUN SHINES DOWN upon the camp once more and the wind is disappearing, the citizens of Ottawa attend the sermons and lectures in goodly numbers. Mrs. E.G. White delivered a fine address on the education of the young, and also spoke in the early morning meeting, and the afternoon praise meeting at the close of the final lecture on church government. The evening lecture on the evils of religious legislation, the particular subject being the recent bill introduced into congress proposing an educational amendment to the constitution, drew out a good audience. Among the new arrivals is Elder O.A. Olsen from England. He is president of the General Conference.

THE FINAL SERMON ON CHURCH GOVERNMENT...

BY A.T. JONES

"1 COR. 13:4 IS WHERE OUR LAST LESSON CLOSED. In another place Paul says charity builds up, this is a building we are studying. In another lesson we read we were to seek the good of others. Thinketh no evil. Who stands blameless in this? None. Well, if all the gifts are nothing to us without charity and charity thinketh no evil why wonder that the gifts are not among us? If all these gifts, with the gifts of God's Son, have developed in us so little appreciation in us how can we expect greater favor? What good would it do us? But if we desire charity, then when these gifts do come, it will do us good, and mark this, when we ask the Father for them He will give to us more abundantly than we can expect. But when we ask Him for the Holy Spirit we ask for the most precious thing the universe affords. Let us not ask them carelessly. The Saviour said all manner of sins should be forgiven, even the sins against the Father and Son, but that there should be no forgiveness for blasphemy against the Holy Ghost. So then when we came to the Lord asking for it, let us come appreciating what we ask for. It is perfectly right to ask for it, but let our minds realize more fully the sacredness of the thing we ask for that we may appreciate it more if it comes, else it would do us more harm than good, as in the case of those who had the gospel without appreciating it. Charity thinketh no evil, not only does not speak but does not think it. Charity is the bond of perfectness, but how natural it is to think evil, to put an evil construction on the words or acts of another. Let us rather strive to learn the burden they carry and help them then to exercise uncharitable thought in reference to them. 'As a man thinketh in his heart, so is he.' If you and I think evil of another, we are evil. If we have impure thoughts, we are impure. Rejoice not in iniquity. Take no delight in wild, wicked, slanderous stories. Rejoice in the truth. Charity never faileth. Now abideth these three, faith, hope and charity. If we have charity, the love of God, then the virtue of that will show itself; the work of His spirit in our heart, if we will aim at that, the Lord will see to it that the gifts of God will follow. It does not follow that because a people have the truth that all these things must go with them. Nor does it follow that if the people have these gifts that Christ is with them. The day will come that some will say to Him, 'Lord, have we not prophesied in Thy name and in Thy name done many wonderful works?' But Christ will not know them, although He does not say they did not do the works.

"If we have charity, the love of God growing in our hearts, all these gifts will follow and Christ will do His work through us, He being our head and controlling and guiding us. Let there then be that harmony and love among us that nothing else will bring except seeing Christ fully. Study Him, and we shall see alike and all will act together in unity. We can not see all things at once at one time. Minds do not all act at the same rate or in the same way, but when one sees the light let him wait patiently until the others see it also. Be not uneasy about another. The Lord is over it all, and nothing can cause shipwreck to the cause of God, or prevent victory and salvation and a glorious triumph for the third angel's message. Go calmly about your work in the peace that trust in Him gives, and all will come out well and perfectly. Lay all the burden and care upon Him, for He careth for you, and it will all come out just right. Why is it that the testimonies say so often to us: 'We have a living Saviour'? It is because we fail to realize that He is alive and that we can go to Him at all times for council and help. Therefore if any of you lack wisdom let him ask of God. Let him ask not wavering. What the soul wants is stability, solidity of character, in full assurance of faith—a belief that God is, and that we can find Him, Hebrews 10:22. Do we believe this? If so let us act it out. He has said, 'I will never leave thee or forsake thee.' Then let us say it boldly, the Lord is my helper and I will not fear what man can do unto me, Hebrews 13:5–6. If we do not believe, does that make His faithfulness of no effect? 2 Timothy 2:11–13. Have we not acted as though we could not tell how God would act. Let us believe He is not variable, but acts the same all the time, James 1:17.

"What are these words written for? That He cannot deny Himself. He is the Rock of Ages. If then we are anchored to Him, if the earth goes out from under us, why underneath are His arms—can anything hurt us? Then trust in Him for what He says. Let us understand then what it is to be joined to Him, that we may have a refuge—which hope we have as an anchor for the soul, sure and steadfast—that we may be as stable as the Rock of Ages itself. What does Paul say? Acts 22:22–24—Paul knew not what was to occur, but he did know that bonds and afflictions awaited him everywhere. What a condition! 'Nevertheless none of these things move me.' There, brethren, was a man anchored to God. All he thought of was finishing his ministry and carrying the gospel. Why was he there? To be a pattern to all who after should believe on Jesus Christ. Then like Him, whatever awaits us let none of these things move us. Life is nothing. Jesus Christ is more than all. Now 2 Timothy 4:6–8. He says 'I am ready to be offered,' His course was finished with joy. The Lord wants His people to be in such a condition of faith and unity that He can accomplish His work through them. Shall we look upon our church as the house of God? That we are temples of the Holy Ghost? Will you carry the feeling home and cheer each other in this way? Christ never failed or was discouraged, and if we find Him for all He is, we shall never fail or be discouraged. We are Christ's body and members of his body and his bones, he feeling pain more than these members we cause pain to, in the church. So if we love Christ we can not hate the brethren or cause them pain. Let us be tender and considerate to the weak and seek to lift them up. If one suffer, let all suffer with him. If one rejoice, let all rejoice with him. The gifts are given according to the strength we have, and He asks returns according to the ability each has, and no other has the right to judge another in it. If he uses the ability Christ has called Him to exercise in His place it is all acceptable to God. The Holy Spirit is given to each to profit with all to be exercised to the glory of God, Christ being in it all, and over all, and all the honor is to be given to Him. Over all the work of the church is charity coming from Christ, and He asks a return to His honor and glory. Brethren, let us be Christians. Let us have that faith that will make Jesus a personal, living Saviour to all of us. According to your faith be it unto you. Just so far as you exercise faith, just so much power of God will you have. For the gospel is the power of God unto salvation. This gospel, then is the greatest power known by man, because it brings to man the power of God, and it comes to us by faith."

SERMON OF MRS. E.G. WHITE

NEARLY 2,000 PEOPLE ASSEMBLED at the tabernacle to hear the afternoon sermon and Mrs. E.G. White's earnest exhortations. The first words of the discourse were drawn out in response to the sentiment of the opening hymn, 'The Old, Old Story," and were followed by an earnest appeal to parents on the proper education of children. Referring to 1 Peter 1:34, she said:

"Should not the old, old story of the resurrection of Christ from the dead be to us one of joy? Many professional Christians go about with their heads down as though Jesus were yet in Joseph's new tomb. He is not there, dear friends, He is risen, and we want to talk of Him, of His love and power to save us from our sins. The story of His love should be to us as much a song of joy as it was to the disciples of old, for we have as much reason to joy in their salvation which His death brought out for us as they. If we take a right view of Jesus we will not be found talking discouragement and gloom. We may gather and appropriate all the promises of God to ourselves. We go into a beautiful garden fragrant with lilies, roses and pinks, and besides these, thistles and briers. We take our eyes from the roses and think of the briers, and complainingly ask, 'What business have these here?' Well, I want to know what business you have to look at or touch them, when there are roses, lilies and pinks to feast the eye on. So the word of God is a garden of beautiful flowers of promise. Let us look on these. Take a flower. As you behold it in the distance it is beautiful. Draw nearer and you are delighted with its fragrance. Examine still closer and you are impressed with the delicacy of its tint and structure which nothing but a God could give it. So with the Bible. In reading its prayers we should leave our minds open to receive new light and should constantly draw so near to God that we can seek for His mercies. We do not want to dwell on the dark side, but rather let memory's walls hang with the beautiful pictures of God's mercy and love. We should train our tongues to sing the praises of God. Have we not enough to praise Him for? He says, what more could I do for my vineyard than that I have done? Sure enough! Has He not given His son! We are not left to battle with the powers of darkness alone. After Jacob had defrauded his brother of the birthright, he was a wanderer. He was a discouraged man as he contemplated his deprivations with the blessings of home, mother—all. But as he lies with his head resting on his pillow of stone, he sees a ladder stretch from the earth to the highest heaven. He saw that in that ladder the gift of heaven was portrayed to man. He said, 'this is indeed the gate of heaven.' It is by this ladder (Jesus Christ) only, that we can climb to heaven. When Adam separated himself from his God it was Christ who bridged the gulf. Suppose the ladder did not connect humanity with divinity by one inch? All would be lost, for of ourselves we can do nothing., But we unite our humanity with Christ's divinity and are drawn up step by step by the cords of God's love.

"Christ is our substitute as one who will fight our battles for us. The human arm of Christ encircles the fallen race and with His divinity He grasps the throne of the Infinite.

"He says, 'Come unto Me for My yoke is easy.' We are to find the rest in bearing the yoke of Christ. Are we wearing the yoke of Christ or have we manufactured a yoke of our own? If you are groaning under your burdens you have not Christ's yoke upon you, for He says, 'My yoke is easy and My burden is light.' But if you wear a yoke of self-righteousness you will find it very heavy. Mothers, are you wearing the yoke of Christ? Home religion is what we want. The fear of God should be taught to our children, and pity and love should circulate through the rooms at our home. Christ touches humanity that He may help us how to be partakers of the divine nature. This is what the parents want in teaching their children to be obedient, respectful, courteous, for this is religion. If you teach them in this way, it will train them to be respectful and obedient to their Heavenly Father. You can teach them from their babyhood to love Christ. Consider the responsibility you bear in training your children. You must mould and fashion them through the aid of the grace of God that they may grow up honorable men and women. Instead of embroidering their dresses, show them that the best adornment is a heart of simplicity and love, that they may grow up with the spirit of Christ. They should be under control of their parents and when they get older they will keep their temper under control. When I see the child that flings itself on the floor in anger my heart aches within me. If they were taken in hand by parents, we would not hear the results of so many outbursts of temper in men, we would not hear of so many church trials. The home should be made cheerful. The best room should not be shut away from the little ones. Make them realize that home is in the best, the cheeriest room in the house. Give them the benefit of sun and air, which is the best doctor. It takes much of the grace of God to raise children. Let them know the mother love, in order to comprehend the love of God. On the Sabbath, do not tie them to the bed post for fear they will not keep the day properly and then sing, 'Lord in Thy Sabbath I delight.' Take them to walk among the trees and in the fields, that show God's creative power, and thus lift them up through nature to nature's God. When 11 years old, I was in despair, my education in regard to the love of God having been neglected. But when I got a view of His love, I never forgot it. I cannot look upon the lofty tree, the spear of grass, or the flower of the field, without thinking of the love of God. We can take our children's hearts and turn them in praise to God as the sunflower turns its petals to the sun.

"Satan has darkened the minds of man and has given them wrong views of God. It is Satan who has given the trouble and trials and wretchedness to the human family. He casts his hellish shadow athwart our path, but we are not to look at him. Take your eyes away and gaze on the lovely form of Christ and contemplate His power and love and all will be right.

"Christ said, 'Consider the lilies,' and etc. Carry your minds back to the glory of Solomon sitting on his throne flanked with golden lions and surrounded by gardens of flowers and all that could make a man happy. Was he happy? No. We hear him moan out: "Vanity, vanity, all is vanity!" It was not a lack of beauty that made unhappy the greatest king that has ever held a scepter. He was an idolater. His career shows him a disappointed man and that riches, power, glory and fame are not sufficient to make a happy man. No, he lacked the peace of God which brings contentment. So teach your children that the beauty of the lily should decorate their hearts. 'Whose adorning let it not be that outward adorning of plaiting the hair, and of wearing of gold, or of putting on of apparel, but let it be the hidden man of the heart, in that which is not corruptible, even the ornament of a meek and quiet spirit, which is in the sight of God of great price.'

"Teach them that it is not the beauty of race, dress, wealth, etc., but the beauty of character that elevates them in the scale of moral value with God. We have solemn responsibilities in the education of our children, that they may have Christian politeness.

"Then let us bring Christ into our own hearts so that our children may have an example of Christ in the home. Let us show tenderness and love and act with God in building up this home religion. Children do not seem to realize or have any sense of the respect that is due the parent any more than the respect due to God. But if you teach them to obey you, they will respect you, and will respect and obey Jesus. When the Sabbath comes to you draw them about you and tell them of the undying love of Jesus, point them to the necessity of entering upon the Sabbath without crowding its holy hours; the necessity of having the houses and faces clean and tidy for the Sabbath, for if the corners of your house are untidy, there will be some dirty corners in the heart. If your children are thus trained they will not be found in saloons and around card tables when they are older.

"God grant that you may seek to be a partaker of the divine nature. Satan has divorced you from Christ and you think he is far off. The gates of heaven are open and the glory of Christ will shine on you if you trust Him. Let us get the simplicity of godliness. Let us sympathize with our children as Christ sympathizes with us. In this way you will win their love, and then you can place the hand of your child, with yours, in the hand of Jesus and give yourselves to him. Let us be Bible Christians and have the salvation which is by faith in the arm of infinite love. We want our households to experience true conversion to Jesus Christ. Then we will talk of the love of God instead of gossiping about our neighbors. We will be educating ourselves to talk faith, to lift up Jesus, who says, 'They that honor Me I will honor.'"

THE CAMP MEETING

Beginning Of The Workers' Meetings At The Adventist Gathering

Arrival of F.E. Belden, Instructor to Canvassers—A Change of Program, and New Lectures Beginning—Sermons by Mrs. E.G. White and Lectures by A.T. Jones—Elder Olson Addresses the Ministers' Meeting—The Children's Meeting Begun—Decorating the Tabernacle—Preparations for Sabbath School.

Special Correspondence of the CAPITAL

CAMP MEETING OTTAWA, KAN., May 15…

THE BEAUTIFUL WEATHER CALLS OUT LARGER AUDIENCES and enables unfinished work to go forward. The committees on decoration are busy with leaves and evergreens for decoration of the Tabernacle. The institute has closed and the worker's meeting inaugurated. Brother F.E. Belden arrived May 13, and begins his instruction to canvassers today. Elder A.T Jones also begins a short course of new lectures on church organization. The last lesson in reporting was given yesterday. President O.A. Olson spoke feelingly in the ministers' meeting yesterday morning. These meetings will continue for some time. The children's meetings began yesterday, at the same hour 8 a.m. The youth's meeting are quite successful. Mrs. E.G. White delivered another sermon in the Tabernacle. The committee on decorations are busy festooning this large hall, and a bevy of sisters are hard at work cutting out frightful looking lions, bears and other wild animals for the kindergarten lesson on "Noah's Ark" next Sabbath. New arrivals constantly, and all is bustle and activity in and about the camp.

THE SERMON ON RIGHTEOUSNESS...

BY A. T. JONES

"THIS MORNING WE WILL STUDY SOME TEXTS that speak to us of faith, what we are to do with it and what it will do for us. Romans 5:1—to be justified is to be accounted righteous and this by faith, Romans 4:5; Romans 3:22. This righteousness is to take the place of all our sins remember. Now see what the Lord will do with our sins, Isaiah 1:18. The latter condition is just the opposite of the first—the sins no matter how deep the color, will be made white as snow. We are to be clothed with white raiment, our scarlet sins to be changed, our filthy stained garments to be changed like wool, white as snow. When we ask to have our sins taken away it is asking to be cleansed. What does it mean to be made white as snow? Mark 9:3. That is the garment that is to be put upon us—whiter than any fuller can make them. This is the blessed promise. Faith says that this is so. Isaiah 44:22. The Lord has paid the ransom by the death of Christ, now He says return unto Me, I have redeemed thee. All the thick, black clouds have gone blotted out, Micah 7:18,19 passeth by the transgression of what? The remnant? Those who keep the commandments and have the faith of Jesus. That is a promise to us. He is fixing them up for Himself. He is taking their sins from them. He delights in treating them better than they deserve. He delights in us when we believe in Him. All our sins are to go in to the depths of the sea, the deepest depth we can conceive of? Is not that a blessed promise? Psalm 103:11,12. Who can conceive the distance of heaven from us, so great is God's goodness and mercy towards us. Don't we want to worship such a Lord as that? Do we want to offend such a God as that? No, we want to be like Him. Now how far is the east from the west? Suppose we walk out looking for the west. How long shall we seek it? Eternally. Then so far are our sins to be from us, as long as we believe it. Have faith then and keep them eternally away from you. Why should we not have peace? Faith then gives us peace. God gives us the Holy Spirit as a seal of His righteousness. We must ask for the Holy Spirit to receive it, Luke 11:9–13. How must we ask? James 1:6; Galatians 3:13–14. The blessing of Abraham was righteousness through faith, Romans 4:21–25. What does God promise us in reference to our sins? They shall be white as snow. Then we are righteous. He says He will blot out the thick clouds of our sins? If we believe it then, we are righteous. By Micah He says our sins shall go into the sea. Do we believe it? Then we are righteous. Our sins are to go from us an eternal distance. Do we believe God can do this? Then we are righteous.

"Now the promises were not, written out for Abraham's sake alone, but for our sakes to whom it shall be imputed, if we believe on Him who raised the Lord Jesus from the dead. Romans 10:10. Then how are we to have righteousness? By faith. Therefore being justified by faith we have peace with

God—now read Galatians 3 again. We receive the seal of it by faith. Another step we want to take when we receive the promise by faith, Romans 5:1–5, we get into the grace of God by faith (whatsoever is not of faith is sin), and we must rejoice. Why should we not? What have we to complain of? What have we to do but rejoice? The Lord is good. Rejoice anyhow. Rejoice in tribulations also, because the Holy Ghost sheds abroad the love of God in our hearts. Don't get a wrong turn here, it is not love for God (though that will be there), but the Holy Spirit puts God's love in our hearts. God gave His Son when man was enmity toward Him, because He loved them, and when His love is in our hearts, they will go out towards mankind in love as His great heart has done. The evidence we want is to have the love of God in our heart. Now Galatians 5:22. How shall we be good? Have the Spirit of God in our hearts. Do we want the other virtues? These are all the fruit of the Spirit of God. We can't have the fruit unless we have the tree—for it is God that works within us both to will and to do of His good pleasure. John 14:21–23. The Lord went away but promised to send the Holy Spirit to manifest Him. Is that not what we learned yesterday? Where do we abide? At our homes. We are sojourning here. 'We will come unto Him and abide with Him.' Ephesians 3:14–21. We begin, then, at the 16th verse, which speaks of the family of God, not two, but only one, some in heaven, the balance on earth—this is a prayer for us that we be strengthened by the Spirit that Christ may dwell with us by our faith. How can we know that which passeth knowledge? Why, only by faith, and then we know it. Now verse 20: Paul could not find words to tell what he wanted to, and failed to express it all. The Lord says He will do all we ask or think. Do we believe it? Then we can get from Him all we ask or think, further, exceedingly abundantly beyond what we can ask for or think, according to what power? The power working within us. And what is this? Our faith. Well, then, that is all the limit put upon God—the power of God being limited only according to the measure of our faith.

"Then, brethren, let us have faith. God is able to do all He promises. Romans 1:16–17. Many do not know what this expression 'from faith to faith' means. We begin with faith, and the exercise of that faith will develop the capacity to exercise faith tomorrow—so that we grow from faith to faith, from today's to tomorrow's—therefore we grow in faith, and from grace, (favor, power with God) to grace, and in knowledge of Jesus Christ, our Lord. Let us exercise our faith then, and it will develop power—the power of God unto eternal salvation. Why, then, should we not rejoice? Now, faith works, Galatians 5:6. Here is where the work comes in, and is the only work acceptable to God, for it is of God, but works without faith are our own. James 2:18. Well, let it do this for it is true, the man who has the most faith will do the most acceptable work to God. Work is of no value except it have faith, and faith without works is valueless. Works will tell the amount of faith we possess, 1 Thessalonians 1:3; 2 Thessalonians 1:11. Now comes obedience. Where? Romans 16:25–26, all made manifest for the obedience of faith—then all short of this faith is sin, that is, 'comes short' of the perfection of the law of God, according to the view of God—not intentional sin, perhaps, but short of the glory of God, and is not obedience—for without faith it is impossible to please God. So, then, our obedience comes in after we have faith, and God's Spirit is dwelling within us. Do you not see now that we have to be made good before we can do good? If then you want to do better, get more of Jesus Christ in your heart. It is all well enough to want to do better, but go first to Jesus to be made better. Romans 1:5, margin, also 1 Timothy 6:12.

"A battle is to be fought and the beauty of it all is there is a victory to be won, 1 John 4:4; mark what 'overcome' means; 'to conquer,' 'veni, vidi, vici.' I came, I saw, I conquered, is what Caesar wrote home to the senate. I came, I overcame, I conquered is the literal translation. Then to overcome is to conquer—but it does not protect from temptation and battles, but it fits us up and enables us to fight, and gives us the victory, all through faith. Is not faith, then, a glorious thing? Ephesians 6:10–18. After having conquered, be able to stand when the battle is over (see margin of verse 13), having the righteousness of God as our armor, and above it all the shield of faith, to not only stop the fiery darts of the enemy, (which if they strike us create a flame within us), but it quenches them—puts them out. Hebrews 2:5 to Hebrews 2:1–3. Paul says Christ partook of our suffering and took upon Him the bondage of death to rescue us from death, and took upon Him our nature that He might be a merciful and faithful High Priest, so that having stood in our place, remember that He stood there before we did, and if we put Him between us and the temptation, it vanishes, and we conquer in Him. That is the shield of faith. Another thing, brethren, the heart is purified by faith and the pure shall see God. Matthew 5:8. It is made pure and kept pure by Him. How is it done? There is no 'how' to faith; but let us read Luke 8:43–48. Why did He not say before this who touched Him? Because the touch of the woman was the touch of faith and drew virtue from Him. Faith reaches out to Christ and virtue comes in response as surely as it did for that woman, and this is not all. Luke 6:19: Touch Him by faith and virtue will come to all and make you faithful, i.e., full of faith.

"Christ was faithful; His faithfulness comes to us in answer to our faith and that makes us faithful. It is only by His obedience that we are made righteous. Then when I have anything to do let my faith reach out to Him and bring faithfulness from Him to enable me to do it. Faithfulness, that only can do it. If we want to be good, let our faith touch Him, and goodness comes to us and makes us good; if we want to be righteous, in answer to our faith, power comes to us and makes us righteous. In answer to our faith as it grows, more and more of His power and goodness will come to us, and just before probation closes we shall be like Him indeed, and then we shall be keeping the commandments of God in fact, because there will be so much of Him in us that there will be none of ourselves there. That is when we get to the place where we keep the commandments of God, and there is the beautiful promise, 'Here are they that keep the commandment of God and have the faith of Jesus!' We must reach that place yet. There is too much self-glorification, too much self-confidence, but let our faith come to Him. Then that is sanctification, that is what the 26th chapter of Acts tells us, verse 18; also John 17:19. That is genuine sanctification. When that comes it will be alright. Get all that kind of sanctification you can. Faith is actually a something, a reality, and when it touches Jesus Christ, in response to it virtue comes from Him and makes us what we want to be. Get that into your minds, brethren, and let us understand what faith is. Let our faith touch Him and draw from Him virtue, goodness, righteousness, and every good and perfect gift will come to us. Then the glory, the praise and the honor is Christ's and let us give it to Him. Then if there be any virtue at all it is Christ's virtue that makes us acceptable to God in any way whatever. A text to sum up this matter is Hebrews 10:37, 38."

A SERMON BY MRS. E.G. WHITE

1 Peter 2:9—"But ye are a chosen generation, a royal priesthood, a peculiar people."

"**THERE IS VERY MUCH SAID HERE TO SHOW** that we should make our deportment correspond to the truth, which we profess. The world has a right to expect this of us. All who profess truth should stand in the position where that truth places them. It is a crime before God for parents to bring into the world, more children than they can properly educate and train. Children must be kept in purity and moral independence before God and man. If God has moved on you by His Spirit it will show itself in your every day life. This is religion. Mothers and fathers, having natural tendencies which are foreign to the readings of the Spirit of Christ, cannot properly arouse the interests of their children so they can sense their responsibility before God and man, as they grow into maturity, unless they have their entire dependence upon God. How many we can recall who claim to have religion but who are not genuine home Christians? The habits of the parents should be neat and orderly, as the children will form their characters largely from the example they set them. There are emanations from the body, constantly, which necessitate scrupulous cleanliness. Garments should be kept clean, and the little wearers be taught that to be untidy is sin. Parents have habits which not only defile their own lives but the lives of their children, and they grow up in wickedness and corruption. Parents, you must preoccupy the garden of your child's heart, you must sow it with seeds of truth and piety. Fence a corner from your garden and watch, for an example, the progress of vegetation. You sow no weeds and cultivate no flowers, but what will be the result in the fall? It will be full of weeds and thistles, Mothers should be, of all persons, the nearest to the heart of the child. You should keep your ears alert to catch their words, and your eyes open to notice their actions.

"Eli was a priest, but though he was a good man, he was too easy with his children, and he did not restrain his boys in their wickedness. What did God say? 'Them that honor me I will honor, and they that despise me shall be lightly esteemed. Behold the days come that I will cut off thine arm, and the arm of thy father's house, that there shall not be an old man in thine house.' So the sin of these children lay at the door of their parents' soul. Brethren and sisters, may it not be so with us? You must look into the habits of your children if you expect to have households that God will honor. Abraham was visited by angels that were on their way to destroy the corrupt city of Sodom. God said He would tell Abraham about the destruction because he has trained his children in a proper manner. Abraham pleaded with God to spare the city for the honest inhabitants, of whom but ten could be found. Here we have an example of a city where the leaven of licentiousness had been at work, and that great city was destroyed. Brethren and sisters, we ought to be wide awake. We need not trust in our own wisdom or strength, but we can, by faith, lay hold on the infinite and of God. When you bow your heads about the table and offer thanks for your daily portion of food, call their minds to the fact that it is Christ who supplies all our necessities. They will then grow up with hearts that will respond in thanks to God for all His gifts and blessings. Fathers, are you setting an example of kindness and Christian courtesy before your child by showing your wife a husband's love? There are thousands of wives and mothers going to their graves every year whose lives have pined away for the lack of sympathy and love. How many husbands there are who come into the home as cold as ice, and if things are not right just murmur and complain, and thus give license to their children to speak words of disrespect to parents. Now Satan is working on the minds of children in a special manner. The earliest principles are those which stay longest by the child. While we are getting our hearts right at this meeting let us not forget the foundation and neglect to bring these truths to the hearts of our children. Another mistake which cause the heart grief and sorrow to parents when children grow up, is the failure to provide employment for the little hands. Satan works with the indolent, and if you do not see that they grow up in industry, Satan will prey upon their tender minds and they will grow up into wickedness.

"Now when we have been studying about the righteousness of Christ, let the light gained shine into the family circles, and while the truths of God are coming to you in mercy and love, may we not appropriate them to our children? Bring the little ones to God and plead with Him for that wisdom which will guide you in molding the minds of the children, and bring religion into our home duties and responsibilities. Do not praise your children

85

by flattery. If praise is merited use modest words of commendation. If they make mistakes do not censure them. Mothers in the kitchen or sewing room and daughters in the parlor at the piano is a reversed order of things. Teach your daughters the pleasures of industry. Show them that exercise in youth will secure that health which is the index to happiness. Do not copy after those who have no standard of morality and Christian worth. But this work must be done in patience and perseverance, with that living faith that takes hold on the strong arm of God. Bring genuine home religion into the lives of your family. If you have home religion you will have neighborhood religion. Your homes may be places where the angels of God will love to dwell. Let reverence be shown for the house of God. Teach Christian politeness and courtesy in the home and we will have churches fit for the indwelling of the Spirit of God, and if you have not this religion of the home, if your children are allowed to disgrace the religion of Christ, you are not fit to belong to the church of God.

"Now let us take right hold of this matter in humility and love and draw these young hearts out to Jesus, that they may see charms in Him. Weave the lessons of Christ into their young minds. When their little arms encircle your neck tell them the old, old story of Jesus' love. When they go astray, go and pray with them and show them how the angels look upon them. But if you do, never go about it in apparent anger. Be what you want your children to be. If they are willful and stubborn, gain the victory over them by gentleness, and conquer them by love."

THE NEW LECTURE COURSE...

A. T. JONES

"THE LESSON WILL BE ON THE CHOOSING OF CHURCH OFFICERS. Who compose the church? The members, those who believe in Christ. What does the Scripture say of the head of the church—Christ? How many masters are there? One. What are the members? All brethren. Who has the superiority? None. The declaration says also: 'All men are created equal.' Then in the church it is much the same as in the government. All, then, have equal rights. Now suppose we here today are Christians, having equal rights, but each works separately. Can matters go on as well as if united? One can chase a thousand, but two ten thousand. This shows the value of unity of purpose and action and of organization, and this is why Christians are brought together into churches. 1 Corinthians 14:40. All is to be done in order, as God is the author of order and not confusion. Titus 1:5. And order is what Christ wants among those who are to perform His work. The church is the house of God, and if disorderly, will not amount to much. The church is the body of Christ. Our human body is organization, and so we find it all through God's creation. Each one has a right to exercise every part of his right in relation to Christ, but it is always the fact that there are certain ones among us that can exercise certain offices for us better than each one separately can do so, and we relegate to them the right to act in our place for the benefit of all, but none lose their rights thereby. If ten kings delegate to one of their number the right to exercise for all the others this office of king, the nine do not cease to be kings, with all their rights and their heirships to the kingdom. If the one selected dies the delegated rights return to the nine, and they can redelegate to another.

"Ye are a royal priesthood and heirs of the kingdom, but in our work, we need the very best kind of organization. Would it be right for the most fitting to step forward and assume the offices? No, there would not be an assenting voice among us here. If one claimed the office, that act would show him to be unqualified. How then, is the one selected? By the common consent, all having a voice in the selection. If, however, one selects one brother, and another chooses differently, does it follow that some should not have a voice in the matter? If, however, the majority select someone, should not the others yield their choice for the good of all? That is the Spirit of Christ, the common weal, or common good. When one is chosen by the many for the place then comes ordination, the laying on of hands, setting apart for office. When this is done we delegate our authority to him, and he represents every one in that place. Then does he become the master of all or the servant of all? The servant, of course. This is the formal bestowal of authority on him. Now, when we do this solemnly before God, should we not respect the authority delegated to him? Should we cast any reflection upon him or detract from his authority, do we not cast disrespect upon our authority delegated to him?

"In the choice of an officer I read Acts 1:15–26 we find the choice of an apostle to fill the place of Judas. They, the members of the church selected two and presented both to the Lord to make a choice for them. The apostle then was chosen by the people, because if they had been so united as to have fixed upon one, the choice would not have been taken to the Lord. Now Acts 6:16. Here again the seven men are selected by the multitude. Even when the Lord chooses a man independent of the brethren He does not let him go to his work until the brethren lay their hands on him, in this recognizing this order in the church. Acts 9:3–15. Here the Lord chose Saul; now Acts 26:15–18, the Lord tells him why He appears to him, to make him a minister and a witness to be sent to the Gentiles, yet Acts 13:14 shows when he was ordained, which was ten years after the Saviour appeared to him, Paul, being all this time among the churches ministering, but not sent to the Gentiles in the broad field until he could go with the authority of the brethren in the church. Again 1 Timothy 4:14. Here the presbytery lay their hands upon Timothy, the church becoming numerous, the elder, the presbytery act for the members. 2 Timothy 1:6."

THE CAMP MEETING

Arrival Of Elder W.C. White
At The Adventist Gathering

The Workers Meeting Well Under Way The Canvassers' Classes
Organized—Successful Social Meeting in the Afternoon
The Sermon on Church Organization Elder A.T. Jones to
Leave for Pennsylvania on the 20th.

Special correspondence of the CAPITAL

CAMP MEETING, OTTAWA, Kan., May 16…

THE DAY HAS BEEN ONE OF ACTIVITY IN THE CAMP, but the lectures have been more of interest to campers than others. As the great camp meeting proper begins next Tuesday the revival efforts began today to have the workers on the ground in a good spiritual condition before the body of the people arrived, that a spirit of consecration might pervade the camp from the beginning of the meeting. Hence but one lecture of instruction was given, the morning one by Elder A.T. Jones, on "The Qualification of Church Officers." The last of this series, the duties of church officers, will be given tomorrow. Six final lectures will follow, three on the subject of "Righteousness by Faith," and three others on "The Evils of Religious Legislation. The elder will not have time to lecture in Kansas City as was hoped for, but will I go direct to Williamsport, Pa. The weather is cloudy and warm but a good attendance at the lectures continues. Elder O.A. Olsen spoke last night, Elder Jones needing rest.

CHURCH ORGANIZATION…

BY A.T. JONES

"THERE ARE TWO CLASSES OF OFFICERS IN THE CHURCH—elders or bishops, being one and the same—and deacons. Phillipians 1:1, Paul speaks here of

88

bishops and deacons only; 1 Timothy 3:1–8, Paul is giving here instructions in reference to bishops, and onward he speaks of deacons showing these are the only officers. There is another word 'Presbyter' which is simply translating the Hebrew word into English. Presbyter means elder, one who is older than another. (Zenophon's account of the retreat of the 10,000 proves this, see the first verse.)

"This Greek word was adopted to correspond with the Hebrew word, and it was the elderly stable men that were chosen. This is the way it started among the early Christians, all of them, nearly, were Hebrews, but as the Greeks began to increase among them they chose a Greek word to mean more clearly the office. *Episcopos*, this word being made up on two words, *Episcopos*—upon—one who watches—a lookout man—on a watch tower—*scopol*—(a military term, the Greeks being a military people and full of military meaning.)—literally one set upon a high place to watch and look about. It is used to distinguish also a scout, to overlook a country in time of war. We are here in an enemy's land, we are soldiers, fighting battles, needing the whole armor of God; a whole company going through an enemy's country. We have to attend to our various duties so we appoint one to be lookout and scout watching the enemy for us. So then, the terms elder, bishop and presbyter are used, but all refer to one and the same person, and though not always the oldest person, yet he had to possess that gravity and stability found in elderly persons. In reference to their military terms, 2 Timothy 2:3; Ephesians 6:11–17. Now in reference to elder and bishop being similar, Titus 1:5–7; Acts 20:17, 28. The word translated overseers is episcopal, the plural, bishops—to watch, oversee, overseers. 1 Peter 5:1,2—feed the flock, taking the oversight. These texts show you plainly that the terms are, as far as the office is concerned, synonymous. Now for the qualifications of a bishop, Titus 17; 1 Timothy 3:3–17; the deacons being required to be the same:

"**First**—'Blameless;' not open to be attacked. Without fault, innocent, guiltless, not meriting censure. Webster—So fully conformed to the rules of right that no one can justly lay blame upon him, or find fault with him.

"**Second**—'The husband of one wife'—not necessarily a married man, but that he shall not have more than one wife. If a man has two living wives, one being divorced, it unfits him for office.

"**Third**—'Vigilant' attentive to discover and avoid danger, or to provide for safety, wakeful, watchful, circumspect; the latter word from *circum*, around, and *specere*, to look, that is to look all round a thing. 'A man who is circumspect habitually examines things on every side, in order to weigh and deliberate.'

"**Fourth**—'Sober,' of sound, well regulated mind, collected, discreet, self-controlled. 'Sober supposes the absence of all exhilaration of spirits, and is opposed to flighty.' One who is 'not wild, visionary, or heated with passion,' but who exercises 'cool, dispassionate reason' in all things.

89

"Fifth—'of good behavior.' Greek *kosmion* from *kesmeo*, 'to adorn, decorate, embellish,' conveying the same idea as in Titus 2:10 'adorn the doctrine.' One who is desirous of order and decorum, modest, orderly, decent and becoming. Conducting himself so as to dignity and be an honor to the position; not exalting or magnifying himself, but exalting his calling and magnifying his office.

"Six—'Given to hospitality,' literally loving strangers 'kind to strangers' 'one who receives and entertains strangers with kindness and without reward.'

"Seven—'Apt to teach'—Skillful in the word of knowledge, so that he may be able to instruct by proofs and show by argument.

"Eight—'Not given to wine'—Siddell and Scott say this means 'the fermented juice of the grape.' One then who does not drink the fermented juice of the grape.

"Nine—'No striker'—Not one who is contentious or given to reproaches.

"Ten—'Not greedy of filthy lucre'—Not a lover of money or of wealth or abundance of any kind, not coveting, close or stingy, but liberal and generous.

"Eleven—'Not a brawler'—Not disposed to fight, not quarrelsome or contentious, not a complainer, not one who scolds.

"Twelve—'But patient'—Reasonable, fair, kind, gentle, yielding.

"Thirteenth—'One who ruleth well his own house, having his children in subjection with all gravity' or as is said to Titus: 'Having faithful children, not accused of riot or unruly.' Because it is explained: 'For if a man know not how to rule his own house, how shall he take care of the house of God?' The distinction between a good home rule and an incompetent one is seen in the description given of Abraham and Eli, respectively, in Gen. 18:19 and 1 Sam. 3:11–13; 2:22–36.

"Fourteenth—'Not a novice'—Not a new convert not one newly come to the faith lest being lifted up with pride he fall into the condemnation of the devil.' If all the company are new converts, put them under a leader until experience is gained.

"Fifteen—'Of good report of them that are without.' The church must have a care for the opinions of those who are outside of the church. Ephesians 5:15. How do his neighbors look upon him (not his faith) as a man and neighbor. Is he neighborly, straightforward, honest?

"Sixteen—'Not self—willed.' Titus 1:7. Yielding to the will or wishes of others; accommodating or compliant; not dogged, stubborn, nor presumptuous.

"Seventeen—'But a lover of hospitality, a lover of good men, sober, just, holy, temperate; holding fast the faithful word as he hath been taught that he may be able by sound doctrine, both to exhort and convince the gainsayers.' Tit. 1:8, 9.

"These are the qualifications which the word of God requires of him who is to be an elder of the church of God, and for deacons the requirements are the same. Further than this, as these officers are filled from among the members, any one of whom may be called to fill them, it follows that God requires every member of his church to have a character in conformity with this description."

THE EVENING SERMON...

BY A.T. JONES

I John 5:4, "And this is the victory that overcometh the world, even your faith."

"FAITH IS VICTORY. THERE IS A WARFARE BEFORE US, a conflict to engage in, but I am glad we may have victory. The eleventh of Hebrews is all on faith and seems to be written with especial reference to Christ's second coming as shown by the last of the preceding chapter. 'For yet a little while and He that shall come will come, and will not tarry,

"We believe that the coming of the Lord is near. We have believed this for a long time, and as time passes and the evidences of this event multiply we are confirmed in this belief, 'that He who shall come will come quickly, and will not tarry.' To the people living at this time it is said, 'now the just shall live by faith.' It is faith that saves, but works come in as the result and fruit of faith. Your faith will be shown by your works. It is the connecting link between God and man. We read the promises of God and become partakers of the divine nature. God speaks, faith claims, and we become possessors of that which God promises, and without it we cannot please God. We cannot honor God with our own ways. Faith is that which takes hold of present truth and acts upon it. There is much that people call faith that is not faith at all. To believe what God has not said is not faith at all. I may believe it but not by faith, because faith must have God's word to rest upon. Abel offered a more acceptable sacrifice than Cain. Cain's was rejected because he did not offer that which expressed a faith in the Christ. Abel brought a lamb, the blood of which was offered in expression of his faith in the blood of Christ. We can worship, we can pray, and not have faith. Noah became heir to righteousness by faith. When the Lord told him that he was going to destroy the world, did it look reasonable? Do you suppose the learned men, the D.D.'s looked upon those things as reasonable? All arose and rejected the message of warning, but on the word of God, Noah built the ark, preached the truth and was saved by faith while those who reasoned were lost. Faith keeps apace with the progression of the truth of God. 'Abraham went out not

91

knowing whither he was going.' Was not that very foolish? He went on a thus saith the Lord. He was just simple enough to do as God commanded, and to believe that when God had more instruction for him he would receive it.

"Moses in the midst of darkness and apostasy stands a monument of his faith. Satan did not want a delivery of Israel, but he cannot hinder the work of God. Although educated in the courts of Pharaoh, Moses chooses rather to suffer the reproach of Christ than to command the riches of Egypt. Unbelief does not make such choices. Moses knew of the promises God had made to the fathers and by faith he cast his life among his own people. So again we see that faith takes hold of the word of God.

"Coming to our own time. A great majority of people in all ages have made the sad mistake of not understanding the times in which they lived. This is shown by the time of Noah and the time of Christ. Christ said on one occasion: 'If thou hadst known, even thou, at least in this thy day the things which belong unto thy peace! But now they are hid from thine eyes because thou knowest not the time of thy visitation.' The Jews prided themselves on being the children of Abraham, the sons of God; yet they did not understand their own time. In their day we would think by the great professions of faith that the world would be filled with it; but we read: 'When the Son of man cometh shall He find faith in the earth?' We trace the lines of prophecy down through Daniel and Revelation, and we find we are always brought face to face with the fact that we are on the brink of the eternal world. This knowledge brings upon every man a solemn responsibility. Most of my audience believe this. Then our works should correspond. Faith is victory. Abel triumphed, and died a martyr to his faith. Noah was victorious, and his faith carried him over the waters of the flood to this side. The Israelites conquered at the Red Sea, by marching straight up to the waters without knowing how they were to pass. God's word never fails. May He forgive us for all our doubting which makes His word a lie.

"If we live in the last days of the world's history, has He a work for this day? He doeth nothing in secret. Turn to Revelation 14:6 and we have three messages. The first angel proclaims the preaching of the gospel to all peoples because of the coming of the day of judgment. The second announces the fall from grace of God's church, and the third angel warning against the work of the apostate power that shall seek to deceive the people of God. What is the nature of this message? 'To every nation, kindred, tongue, and people.' Has this message been given? In 1844 we have the work of William Miller and others heading out in this country the work of Irving and Wolf in Europe, and in all countries we find the same work done. In northern Norway we find people who remember well the preaching of that time from this text. In Denmark we find the same. So the whole world has received the message. Afterward comes the second message: 'Babylon is fallen.' All acknowledge this to be the fall of the popular churches and the coldness and corruption of the churches. Take the third message and we find the prophecy of the making of an image to the papacy. We have preached this for forty years, and the time was when people laughed us to scorn for doing so; for preaching what we now see fulfilling in the national reform movement. Our own presence here tonight proves the fulfillment of that prophecy which says: 'Here are they that keep the commandments of God and the faith of Jesus.' To deny this truth is to deny your own existence. The gospel of the kingdom must be preached in all nations as a witness; then shall the end come. The same work which is going on in this country is going on in Europe, and we there witness the power of the truth. In Russia the work is going on in spite of their stringent awe. God is in this work and may we believe it. But we are not to the end yet. There are millions that have not received the good news of salvation. When I sense it, I say, 'God, tarry yet a little time, that these souls may be warned.'

"Noah, in the eyes of the world, built a monument to his folly when he built the ark, but he believed God, and I thank God for his faith. His faith deserves an eternal monument. We want more missionary spirit, that we may act like living men, living Christians, real and genuine. We want the victory, and pray that we may be faithful. God help us to be faithful, and to consecrate all to the work of God. Let us have some of the consecration of the martyrs and be ready to lay all on the altar of God. Shall we not make the truth we believe a living reality? We have a warning to give; many of us have labored, prayed and sacrificed for the work, but let not our courage fail till our ark is built. May God help the work and bless the people in Kansas, that with others we may at last come off victorious."

THE CAMP MEETING

The Children's Meetings Begin With Capt. C. Eldridge Present

The Canvassers' Classes at 9 a.m., and 5 p.m.—Mrs. White to Address the Ministers and Their Wives Every Other Afternoon at 5 o'clock, Speaking to the Public Alternate Afternoons at 2:30— The Conference will Convene for Business Next Tuesday.

Special Correspondence of the CAPITAL

CAMP MEETING, OTTAWA, KAN. May 17...

THE NEW PROGRAM FOR THE WORKERS' MEETING went into effect today. There will be two classes daily for canvassers, mornings at 9 a.m., and in the afternoon at 5 p.m. The children's meetings will be at 9 a.m., the first being held this morning. Captain C. Eldridge has written he will be here tomorrow. The regular preaching and lecture service will continue as before 9 a.m., 2:30 and 3 p.m. until next Tuesday, the opening day of the camp meeting. Mrs. White addresses the public every other day at 2:30 and on those days the ministers hold their " council" at 5 p.m. Alternate days Mrs. White will occupy the 5 o'clock hour in talks to the ministers and their wives. The conference will convene for business Tuesday morning. There have been no special meetings so far except the usual ones of the auditing committees preparing for the conference. The camp was redistricted today temporarily. It will be finally districted next Tuesday. Decorating the tabernacle progresses nicely and will be completed before the Sabbath.

Elder W.C. White is occupying the afternoon hour in object lessons on—

KEEPING THE COMMANDMENTS

"**2 CORINTHIANS 5:17**. We have seen how we are brought into Christ, and now this says if any man is brought into Christ he is a new creature.

Galatians 6:15; 5:6, nothing avails but this, and faith that works by love of God, being made a new creature by faith, Romans 5:1,2,5; 1 John 5:3—then keeping the commandments comes in after we are new creatures, so then we must be made good, be made righteous, before we **can** do good or do righteousness; 1 Corinthians 7:19—that is the aim set before us in Christ Jesus. Ephesians 2:3—10. We are created unto good works; made new creatures in Him, His righteousness counting for our unrighteousness.

"The good works God's creatures are created in Christ to do are the good works we could not do before. So a new creature will aim constantly to keep the commandments. James 2:1,9. We do not have the faith of Christ with the transgression of the law. Christ did not come to set us free from that, because if we turn from a single point of the law our faith will not avail. But our intent is accepted and ignorant sins are forgiven, yet willful refusal to accept points of truth presented will cause us to lose all the righteousness we ever had. This explains the fast growing evil in the popular churches of today. Years ago the churches were religious—even when the third angel's message started they were accepted of God, but when they refused to comply with the requirements of the message, then they lost all the righteousness they had and have had to invent all manner of means by which to keep the congregations together, by entertainments. This is the philosophy of the degeneration of the churches. James 1:14. No more does faith profit unless it is kept alive by these works. God has provided, James 2:18, let us show our faith by our works. Faith is the anchor that holds the craft in the right place to work, and the storms beat us nearer home. Verses 21–23. Abraham was counted righteous when he believed and without works, the other righteousness came in twenty-five years after, so he was not counted righteous by works, that Scripture was spoken when he believed and more than twenty-five years after James says the Scripture was fulfilled. If he had refused to offer Isaac, his former righteousness would have disappeared, so the obedience of his faith completed his righteousness that he had by faith, then our keeping of the commandments is not to become righteous, but because we are righteous.

"Romans 8:26 shows that we cannot even pray right, but the Spirit does it for us, so our prayers are acceptable only through the intercession of Christ and the merits of His blood. Revelation 8:3, 4. Here is the intercession in the sanctuary making intercession for us and God looks upon Christ, his wounds and His sacrifice, and accepts them. Christ was perfect before He came to earth, and His absence makes our prayers acceptable, God imputing His prayer for us to us. How is His righteousness imputed to us? Are our acts righteous as far as they go and is His righteousness applied to finish out the work? No. Christ's righteousness starts at the beginning and makes the action what it ought to be. Romans 1:16. Is not our faith greater than when we came here? Do we not see more of His righteousness than we did? How is it we have more faith and see more of His righteousness? Why, our faith has grown. So it is day by day. We came daily for greater supply of faith. And

95

we finally have so much of Christ's divine nature in us that we can draw the bow strongly enough to hit the mark, and then we will be keeping the commandments of God. Then is it not Christ's work from the beginning and all His divine power? Where, then, do our works come in? Nowhere. Why then do we strive so hard to keep the commandments, if it avails not? It is only by faith in Christ that we can say we are Christians. It is only through being one with Him that we can be Christians, and only through Christ within us that we keep the commandments—it being all by faith in Christ that we do and say these things. When the day comes that we actually keep the commandments of God, we will never die, because keeping the commandments is righteousness, and righteousness and life are inseparable—so, 'Here are they that keep the commandments of God and faith of Jesus,' and what is the result? These people are translated. Life, then, and keeping the commandments go together. If we die now, Christ's righteousness will be imputed to us and we will be raised, but those who live to the end are made sinless before He comes, having so much of Christ's being in them that they 'hit the mark' every time, and stand blameless without an intercessor, because Christ leaves the sanctuary sometime before He comes to earth.

"Now some say, 'I will live better; I will try to build myself up into that place where God can accept me.' If a child tries to do something to build up himself that you may think more of him, and fails, you say it was selfishness and pride, and serves him right; but if a child tries to do something simply to please you, even though bunglingly done you commend him and praise him. So with us if we strive to please our God, no matter how bunglingly we do it, He is so glad to put Christ's righteousness upon us and all heaven rejoices over it. How often a child tries to help mother and she lets it go on, although mother has to do it all over again—yet she delights in the effort of the child to please her. Now like as a father pitieth his children so the Lord pitieth them that fear Him.

"So then we can say with David: 'I delight to do thy law, oh, my God.' Why? Because the love of God was shed abroad in his heart. Now let me read a few texts about pleasing God? Hebrews 11:6. The aim of faith is to please God, because He is so good. Romans 8:8. Again, 2 Corinthians 5:14. The love of Christ draws us and we get that love through faith. But can we love God if we cannot keep the commandments of God? No. We can do neither until we become new creatures. 1 John 3:21–22. Now let us read Colossians 1:9–10. We should be able to walk pleasingly before Him. 1 Thessalonians 4:1. This, then, is the root and motive in keeping the commandments to please God, and not to make ourselves righteous. God makes, and keeps us righteous and then we keep the commandments to please God who has done so much for us. As then it is the power of Christ through which we keep the commandments now, and it will be His power through which we shall live forever in the new earth, His name to us is what? Jeremiah says it is 'The Lord our Righteousness.' Jeremiah 23:5–6. "

THE CAMP MEETING

A Stormy Day Interferes With The Classes And Lectures

Captain C. Eldridge, Present—No Attempt Made to Give an Afternoon Lecture because of the Storms—The Minister's Council Utilizes the Large Eighty-Foot Tent—The Assembly Room Filled With New Arrivals Waiting for a Chance to Pitch Their Tents.

Special Correspondence of the CAPITAL

CAMP MEETING, OTTAWA, KAN., May 18...

C AMP MEETING, OTTAWA, KAN., MAY 18 has rained heavily during the night and nearly all day. The morning lecture was given in the tabernacle under difficulties, the rain on the tin roof drowning the speaker's voice at intervals, and the cold wind chilling the persons of the auditors. No attempt was made to deliver the afternoon lecture, the rain coming down steadily. The large assembly room was not available for lectures, it being necessary to give it up to new comers who could not erect tents because of the incessant rain. These have divided the large room into compartments, using the pieces of their tents for walls. The ministers retreated to the 80-foot circle tent, used for youth meetings to hold their 5 o'clock council. Many new arrivals and the committee are puzzled to care for them. All the rented cottages and houses are full, and some of the visiting brethren will, it is said, be quartered in the neighboring hotels. The early 5 o'clock and the district social meetings, Sabbath (Saturday) morning will not be held on account of the cold and rain. The tabernacle was covered in on one side (it being a piece of ground roofed over simply, without sides) by the canvas sides of some large tents not yet pitched and a space capable of seating about 1,000 persons shielded from the cold wind, where services were held at sundown, and preaching service at 8 o'clock, Elder W.S. Hyatt, of Texas, officiating, it being thought best to discontinue the regular course of lectures until the weather clears again, that the citizens of Ottawa may be able to hear them.

THE LECTURE ON CHURCH ORGANIZATION...

BY A. T. JONES

"THE SUBJECT IS THE DUTIES OF CHURCH OFFICERS and the qualifications that are necessary for an elder more especially in connection with the word *episcopos*. Paul refers to this somewhat in Hebrews 13:7. There are no rulers in the church but there are guides, see margin. The marginal writing is more in harmony with the meaning of *episcopos* than ruler. It will be better to use this with the marginal readings, as the elder is a 'scout' sent to watch for them in the camp. One form of duty there is, is to watch for souls—so in the seventh verse 'conversation' here refers to our whole course of life, this being the meaning of the word in Paul's time. Then the whole purpose in choosing an elder was to obtain a guide into the way of life to lead us to Jesus. Acts 20:28 conveys this idea the same as Peter in 1 Peter 5:1–2. Notice the margin of the third verse with the word 'oversee' in the second verse. It is not to overrule but oversee, to care for. Here both authors use the word to feed the flock, the figure implying a shepherd, so verse 4, Christ is called the chief shepherd, and we must be under shepherds not to abuse but to feed and care for the flock. This is another view from the one in the previous lesson. There the elder was shown as a vigilant watchman, the soldiers' aid. In these references today we find him the minister of the fold, the shepherd, that is, under shepherd. Peter having had experience as one, John 21:15–17. Why did He ask Peter three times? No doubt because he denied Him three times, yet the lesson here, for us, I think, is this, that before we attempt to feed the flock be sure we love Christ, else we cannot feed the flock, we may rule or scold them but not feed them. If the elder loves Christ, his service will feed the flock, 2 Cor. 5:14, the love of Christ constraining us, then what we do will accomplish good. If this love does not constrain us, our acts are selfishness. The next verse shows this to be so. If love of Christ constrains us, then our acts are pleasing to God, otherwise we please ourselves simply.

"Now, Peter tells us that when the Chief Shepherd shall appear we shall receive a crumb, so we are under shepherds and must study the Chief to know Him to act in His place. Luke 15:3–7. Here we have the method of the Chief Shepherd, then when an undershepherd sees one of the flock going astray he should leave the rest and seek for it. Is it any excuse then, for an elder to allow anything of a temporal or other nature to excuse him from his duty? John 10:11. The Good Shepherd gave His life for His sheep, then should not that spirit animate the undershepherd? If so, the place for him is where the lost sheep is. Is it right, then to leave all this work until the quarterly meeting, and then appoint committees to go and investigate? This is the elder's work, and he is not put in office to appoint committees for this duty. Verse 10, 11.

"In 1 Samuel, chapter 17, we find a record here of David coming to the camp before which Goliath stood defiantly. David wished to slay him and his brothers try to restrain. him, but he tells them about killing a lion that had stolen a lamb, and David pursued and killed him; so also he killed a bear. Boy, as he was, stood face to face with a lion, jeopardizing his life for his lamb, holding the fierce beast by the beard while he struck him. There are not many men who would battle for a lamb like that. Now what has God said about this man? Psalm 78:70–72. That because of the care David gave to his sheep, God said he wanted him to rule over his people instead of the fickle king Saul, passing by the other noble looking sons of Jesse to select the humble shepherd boy, saying to the prophet, 'Rise and anoint him for I have chosen him.'

"Isaiah 40:11. This is what the True Shepherd did, and it was David's gentleness that commended him to God. There is a good deal in this, that 'the sheep know my voice.' If the flock hears the tones of the Good Shepherd in one voice it will be easier to lead them than it has been to drive them. John 10:4,7. Let us have the tones of the Good Shepherd, then we can go before them and they will follow.

"Now I read Psalm. 23. David tells here how the Chief Shepherd treats him, not keeping him always in one pasture, but leading him into fresh ones, tender, new grass. So an elder wants to study, to be apt to teach, apt to show by argument, so as to have something fresh for food always, then there will be greater prosperity in the work. Not that he should preach a sermon every time, only a few texts or words, perhaps, to lead out their thoughts into new channels. Do not get into a routine. Every member should make this a matter of thought and try to help the elder by watching the line of his discourse or talk, and in the social meeting lead out in that line. Then a good meeting will follow—a special meeting, not a strangers' meeting. Besides, if we are in sympathy with the speaker, not criticizing or finding fault, we can obtain great benefit from any sermon or talk. We may be perfectly familiar with the text but if the Spirit of the Lord directs him, those texts never fall together in his mind, as they would in ours, and so help and new thoughts will come to us; besides, it helps him in giving him the benefit of the closeness of our sympathy with him. If we withhold this we weaken him. The elder of the church is to visit the afflicted ones and lead them into quiet water; instill faith into the discouraged and lift up the fallen, because that is what the Good Shepherd said. 'Learn of Me.' Paul and Peter write the elders to lead the flock into the paths of righteousness. So also in the shadow of death, to go as far as they can and leave the dying one in the hands of the Good Shepherd, to meet him again hereafter. To take also the Bread of Life and prepare a table at which the flock can feed, and then if they do all they can to see that goodness and mercy surround the flock, they shall have peace. Then let us all get in that place in which, when the words of the Good Shepherd are heard, we may recognize His voice. There are thousands of people in the church today who are weary of the Word as spoken to them and do not know what to do, but as soon as we get into that position where God can see us, the Lord will call these out to hear the truth."

THE CAMP MEETING

The Third Sabbath In Camp—
An Interesting Kindergarten

The End of the Storm and a Sunshiny Sabbath—The Swollen
Marais de Cygene Campers Occupy all Vacant Rooms Another
Supply of Tents Telegraphed for—Several Hundred People
Expected this Week—The Main Meeting to Begin Today—The
Sermons and Lectures Resume and a Fair Attendance
from Ottawa Report of the Sabbath School
—Another Storm at Night but Fair Weather Sunday.

Special Correspondence of the CAPITAL

CAMP MEETING, OTTAWA, KAN., May 20...

T HE DARK CLOUDS BROKE AWAY during the night and the sun came out clearly
Saturday. By noon it was comfortably warm again; the mud dried up
and the water disappeared rapidly so that the picnickers ate their dinner
seated on the grass of the lawn, but the swollen stream, the Marais de Cygne,
(which has risen over seven feet in twenty-four hours) carrying on its bosom
the logs and debris captured by its overflowing waters is still a reminder of
the fierce storm that has passed.

A very large number of new faces are met with and it is estimated that
there are 400 in camp now. All the tents are full and all the vacant rooms
in the neighborhood have been rented and are now occupied. A telegram
has been sent to Kansas City for an extra supply of family tents. It is feared
that it will not be possible to pitch them in time for the newcomers that
are expected to pour in this week, the general camp meeting beginning on
May 21. The camp grocery man has opened up his stock of goods and expects
to supply all the campers who "keep house." Tea, coffee, tobacco and pork,
however, he does not keep, there being no demand for such articles among
Seventh-day Adventists. Elder Olsen preached the morning sermon, Mrs.
E.G. White addressed the afternoon meeting and Elder A.T. Jones lectured in

the evening. Mr. C.H. Parsons, vice president of the Kansas Sabbath School Association and his mother arrived from Topeka Friday last and will remain to the close of the meeting. The youths' meeting will be at 5 and 10:30 a.m., hereafter. At the Sabbath meeting thirty-six testimonies were born in thirty minutes. A heavy rain with hail came in the evening and services were suspended until its close. Sunday was clear and warm.

THE SABBATH SCHOOL

THE THIRD SABBATH SCHOOL HELD in connection with the campmeeting, was in point of numbers attending, in scholarship, and in interest, in advance of the others. The total attendance was 350. There were fifty-four classes formed, of which six belonged to the intermediate and primary department with twenty-three scholars, nine kindergarten with fifty-five scholars and thirty-nine seniors with 272 scholars. The donations were $10.53 against $8.31 last Sabbath. The superintendent was Elder S.J. Rossean, president of the Kansas Sabbath School Association, with C.H. Parsons, vice president, as assistant, and the following corps of division superintendents: J.A. Morrow, O.S. Ferron, P.P. Wilcox, Emma Rossean, with fifty-four teachers, and Miss Lucy M. Olds, secretary and treasurer of the Kansas Sabbath School Association as the superintendent in charge of the kindergarten. The review of the senior division was conducted by Elder W.N. Hyatt, president of Nebraska Sabbath School Association; the intermediate by Elder W.S. Cruzan, president of Texas Sabbath School Association; and the primary by Mrs. C.P. Haskell, of Denver, Colorado.

This last review was extremely interesting. The lesson was upon the flood, particularly the building of the ark, and its occupation, etc., and, as noticed in the CAPITAL for the 16th, the ladies of the Sabbath School Association connected with kindergarten work led by Miss L.M. Olds had been busy throughout the week making new sets of pasteboard animals, birds, etc., in pairs or sevens according to whether they were "clean or unclean." A herculean task well accomplished. The marvelously and wonderfully formed beasts and birds, as they stood up in their allotted places in the black arks that nearly covered the surface of the Lilliputian tables no doubt were gazed upon with feelings of admiration by the little ones who, seated in their diminutive chairs around the table, listened with solemn awe and interest to the wonderful story of God's dealing with unrepentant sinners, and justification of the righteous. In the review of the day's lesson Mrs. Haskell briefly outlined the lesson of the previous Sabbath, the Bible account of Enoch, the righteous one whom God took to Himself, not letting him taste of death, as an introduction, and passing rapidly to the story of the building of the ark and the collection of the birds and beasts, and their entry into the huge vessel accompanied by Noah and the other seven, closing out the coming of the angel who shut the door. The animated faces of the little ones and the quick response to questions asked, showed the attention paid to the instruction given by the patient teachers, and interest excited by the story as told by Mrs. Haskell. It is hoped that the workers who prepared the articles needed for this lesson felt repaid for all their toil by the impressions made upon these young and tender minds There were over thirty teachers, superintendents and other workers in Sabbath school, who occupied seats in the rostrum specially provided for them, who came purposely to study the methods adopted, all of whom seemed to gain valuable hints and instruction in reference to and their application to kindergarten work. It is with no slight satisfaction that we notice among teachers the growing interest in Sabbath school work for the children and youth, and the earnest desire manifested to improve in methods of teaching and range of subjects for study.

THE EVIL EFFECT OF SUNDAY LAWS...

A.T. JONES

"WE WILL PRESENT TONIGHT THE SUBJECT OF SUNDAY LAWS, and learn if there is any good basis for them—tonight taking up the civil side of the question. It is claimed that one day of rest is for the public good, and for that purpose it would be right for states to legislate upon it. But this is a mistake.

"First, to compel men to do no work is to force them to be idle, and, kept up continuously, enforces a great deal of idleness, and this is the root of untold evil, being a proverb in many languages that 'Satan finds some mischief for idle hands to do.' Idle men will always find something to employ themselves about in place of their lawful occupation.

"The knights of Satan are complaining greatly against employing prisoners for manufacturing purposes because they say it tends to degrade and bring down the price of free labor, and in some places, New York, for instance, they are powerful enough, and have induced the legislature to prohibit this class of labor. I read from the *New York Independent* the following, as showing the result of this action. I read from its issue of April 18,1889, the statement of Warden Dunston of Auburn prison: 'The enforced idleness of the convicted criminal demoralizes his mental and wrecks his physical system.' Warden Fuller of Clinton prison says: 'To avoid the debilitating effects, mental, moral and physical, that are the sequel to the confinement of prisoners in their cells without occupation, and in answer to the personal appeal of the men for work, I have made for them such employment as I could.' Warden Brush of Sing Sing says; 'Idleness in a prison is horrible to contemplate, especially to prison officials, who understand fully its consequences, the prisoners soon become restless, unhappy and miserable. Time with them passes slowly; their bodies soon become unhealthy, and the mind must become diseased. In fact, nothing but disease, insanity and death can be expected from this condition.' Physician Barber of Sing Sing prison says: 'Confinement in their cells five-sixths of their time in almost solitary idleness appears to be forcing them back upon themselves–a prey to the baneful influences of impure thoughts, corrupt conversation, disgusting personal habits, physical and mental prostration, and moral degradation.' General Superintendent of Prisons Lathrop says: 'Idleness is the bane of a prison, whose malign influence no prison administration, however humane, ingenious and energetic, has ever been able to overcome.' Further, I have a letter from the warden of Sing Sing prison in which he says: 'In my experience nothing can be so bad in a prison as idleness. I consider it a crime on the part of the state against the prisoners, great wrong to the taxpayer and to society. It is a crime against the prisoner as it totally unfits him for life in the world upon his discharge.

"Industry in a prison means that when a prisoner is discharged he has for capital good health, sound mind, trained muscles, habits of industry, and a trade. And more than this, he has the knowledge that he can earn a living for himself and family. On the contrary, if he is kept in idleness in prison, he must go out a wreck of a man both physically and mentally, with no good habits and no ability to earn a living.' It is of course worse in a prison than elsewhere, yet the effect of idleness anywhere is the same; they will find some kind of employment for the mind and body–so the entire people, if idle, will do. Another illustration is the degradation of the monks of the fourth century, who worked as little as possible. To read of the vice, lasciviousness and degradation of these men is enough to convince anyone of the evils of enforced idleness. Now it is well known that Sunday is the worst day of the week for wickedness, crime and drunkenness, worse than all the rest of the week put together. These who are working for a Sunday law claim this is because the saloon is open, but is it a fact that saloons are open as freely on Sunday as on other days? No. Why then is it that more wickedness is committed on Sunday? Is it not because more men are idle on Sunday than on any other day? That it is not the saloon is apparent, but that it is because idleness prevails among a greater number is conclusive. I read now from Dr. Craft's work 'The Sabbath for Man.' 'That nearly half the drinking and three-fourths of the drunkenness of this country takes place on Saturday evening and Sunday is too notorious to need proof or illustration.' That is the time for compulsory idleness. It is not then the opening of the public houses but the increased idleness. I read now from Professor Swing in regard to Chicago:' To have twenty-five hundred saloons open on any day of idleness is not only to rob the day of its prime quality, of its physical and mental use, but it is to transform the day into a positive evil. It is no advantage to common people to have a day of rest from common labor if the day is to bring an unusual outlay of money and an inflammation of the passions.'

"'How are they going to prevent the outlay of money and the inflaming of the passions, then, if they compel them to be idle? If the stores are closed, and the manufactories are closed, and the spade and the pick are put aside for twenty-four hours, only that glasses and bottles may rattle, and cards be shuffled, and dice cast, and hard earned money be wasted, then it would be better that industry should rule all the seven days of the week.' Precisely. How then are they going to cut off the card playing? A man can gamble at home as well as in a saloon. The man that has gambling in his mind will do so. 'Regular labor all through the year would not injure a laboring man half as much as he would be injured by fifty-two days in the beer shop. A day which shuts a factory and opens a saloon is an absurdity. What a sweet day that must be when it is an open question whether those who are to enjoy it will live over it! A broken head is more probable than a saved soul.' This has always been the case from inception of the first Sunday law and will always be so where men are compelled to be idle. 'Statistics show that in Germany, where Sunday liquor-selling is open and untrammeled, fifty-three percent of the crimes are committed between Saturday and Monday morning. Many a poor German woman dreads to have Sunday come. Her husband who has worked hard and kept sober through the week finds it a much more perilous affair on his weekly respite, and returns home from his Sunday recreation in no favorable mood for domestic peace.' Then don't you see that the tendency of all Sunday laws is evil and always must be so? Speaking of England, the author quotes one of the Homilies: 'It doth too evidently appear that God is more dishonored and the devil better served on the Sunday than upon all of the days of the week besides.' Similar testimony Dr. Crafts says, is given by judges, chaplains and others of the effect of the Sunday liquor traffic in the United States. The records of the Brooklyn police courts showed that on Sunday there were twice as many arrests for drunkenness and disorderly conduct as on any other day of the week. Almost any Monday morning he (Reynolds) was waited upon by the wives of laborers who had been arrested for Sunday sprees, and asked to use his influence in their favor.

"If there were prohibition laws there would not be as much of this, but the evils of enforced idleness would be apparent anywhere. In the face of all this evidence I appeal to any honest, fair minded man if it would not be better to allow men to follow their honest callings than to subject them to all the evils and temptations of an idle Sunday? 'Sunday liquor selling,' says Dr. Crafts, 'Is the pirate of commercial life, preying upon all other trades and interests. On Sunday it robs the church and the home of the presence of fathers and brothers.'

"Dr. Crafts cited London as the best evidence of good from an enforced Sunday observance, and Senator Payne of Ohio, at the hearing before the committee having charge of the Sunday rest bill, asked him this question: 'Have you seen the statement lately made by authority that London on Sunday is the most immoral and dissipated city in the world?' And Dr. Crafts replied: 'That is due to liquor drinking, not to the fact that mails are closed.' Now these men go about to reform this state of things by creating more idleness. Is it not plain that no state can afford to have Sunday laws, and enforce them? 'Why,' says one, 'is not a town better that keeps Sunday than one which does not?' Yes, but is it the religion that town has, or the Sunday that makes the difference? Is there any religion in a Sunday? Is it not the respect the people have in their hearts that makes the difference? Further than all this, a man can on Sunday hire a livery team and race over the streets, get drunk, and do what he will, if he does not become too noisy or unruly, and go free, but an honest man who follows his daily occupation is arrested and fined. What does this do? It puts a premium on crime, does it not? Well then, no state can afford to declare as crimes any honest labor, and put premiums on crime. No Sunday laws then can be beneficial. But does not this argument reflect upon the Almighty in appointing a day of rest? No: God's purpose was that man might worship Him. It is this religious sanction that He has put upon it that forever tends to preserve it from becoming a day of idleness. God has established it as a memorial of Him, and to call man's mind to Him. It is to be kept holy not civilly. Further, man's physical needs are not considered in it at all. We are to work six days because God did so, and rest the seventh day because He did; not for us to rest because it may endanger our health, but we work and rest because the Lord did so, and not because man needs 'one day in seven for physical rest.'

"Man's spiritual needs are all that are considered in the commandment. But when a state forces men to rest on Sunday, not being able to attach to the day the sanction that God attaches to His Sabbath it becomes simply a day of idleness and wickedness. Dr. Crafts said to the Knights of Labor in Indianapolis, in reply to the question: 'Could not this weekly rest day be secured without reference to religion?' 'A weekly day of rest has never been permanently secured in any land except on the basis of religious obligation.' Joseph Cook says: 'You will in vain enforce the day of rest unless you enforce also the worship.' Dr. Crafts says: 'I have received written answers from about one hundred and fifty persons, many of them manufacturers, to the following question: 'In your observation of clerks, mechanics and other employees, which class are in the best physical and mental condition for the renewal of business on Monday mornings, those who are church-goers, or those who spend the Sabbaths in picnics, and other pleasures?' The answer is 'churchgoers.' The churchgoers are worth 25 per cent more on an average. The Sabbath observers and churchgoers, whether laborers, mechanics, merchants, or professional men are in better condition to enter upon work on Monday morning than those who spent Sunday in pleasures of even a comparatively innocent kind. Churchgoers can be recognized in a crowd–clean, healthy, prosperous.' Now if Sunday laws are defensible for health, then only those who go to church get the benefit. Now if this proves anything, it proves the right to force a man to go to church. So then all their arguments go to prove that worship and religion must go with the Sunday law or it becomes a worse day than any other. What will come then? The state will furnish to the church the power to compel men to worship to save them from the effects of idleness. This is exactly what happened in the fourth century, and here comes in another source of evil. It multiplies hypocrites and gets the people into a habit of meanness and dishonesty, so that every way they turn, every step they take only increases the wickedness, and must eventually bring on a train of calamity they little dream of.

THE LAST LECTURE ON CHURCH ORGANIZATION...

BY A. T. JONES

"IN CLOSING MY LECTURES ON CHURCH ORGANIZATION I wish to give some final texts on the duties of deacons, Romans 16:1, the word 'servant' is deacons-a deacon being the servant of the church, Acts 6:1-4. This refers to Acts 4:32-37. These seven (Acts 6) are not here plainly called deacons, but they were really the first deacons ever chosen, the contest showing that they were selected to attend to the details of the church wants, temporal affairs, and to relieve the elders. The root of the Greek word means or signifies 'made dusty by running'—so continuously doing errands that he gets covered by dust. He looks out for the Lords Supper, the robes for baptism, etc. looks after the poor and takes charge of the poor funds, but he does not baptize, that being a part of the duty of the minister. As to administering the ordinances, that is, taking charge, it is customary for the elder to have charge, but in handing out the emblems, the deacons assist, as in the ordinance of the Lord's Supper.

"Another part of church order I wish to notice: Matthew 18:15-18, 'If thy brother trespass against thee, go and tell him.' Is not that a plain statement? Tell who? Him. What further? Alone. Have we been doing this? Have we not been telling other people? Yes, and that is what makes all the church trouble. We have no right to tell a fault to anyone but the brother and, as a last resort, the church. If this Scripture was followed there could be no ordinary church trial. That Scripture was put there to be obeyed, now let us decide to do so hereafter, and that we will never speak of a brother's fault except to him, and that twice before carrying it before the church. What do we tell it to him for? To condemn him? No, to recover him. If he trespass against me, who is hurt? Is it not I? But who is sinning? Is it not he, and is not he the one that is to be saved from the error of his way? We are to tell him to recover him from his fault, and this is the sole object, Galatians 6:1. Who is to restore him? 'Ye which are spiritual.' Then what is to be done first? To see if I am spiritual, whether I have the mind of God or not, and further by the time I go to the Lord I may find out the fault is on my side and I may not have to go to the brother at all, till, if after this, I find the brother is wrong, then I go, in the spirit of meekness, which is Christ's spirit.

"When he shows a person his fault, it is to save him, and that is all the purpose anyone should have in telling another his fault, 'considering thyself also lest thou also be tempted.' There is no room then to go to a brother to find fault with him. Remember, too, we must always make a distinction between the sinner and the sin. 'Hate the sin with all the heart, but the sinner love.' Who can hate sin more than the Lord, yet who loves the sinner more? If we despise the sinner for his sin the Lord will leave us some day to fight the same sin in our own strength and learn our own weakness. Now after telling a brother his fault and he will not hear thee, take with thee one or two more. What for? That they may be witnesses, as the matter may come before the church, and 'every word must be established,' and that by witnesses you can show that the word of the Lord has been followed. What was the idea throughout? To get the brother to see his fault. Now the brethren taken are not to know for what purpose they are called. If I tell it first to them, I give it a coloring of my own. Now these witnesses hear me speak it again to him, and if neither he or they can see it in my light, it is time for me to stop, but if they try to have him see it as I do, and he will not, then let the church hear the matter, and if then he still refuse, 'then let him be to thee as a heathen and a publican'—not to cast him off forever, but to work for him as you would for any other heathen. Paul speaks of this in Titus 3:10—a heretic being 'one who chose for himself.' If then a brother withstands you and your witnesses, and the church, to choose for himself and is a heretic, 'being condemned of himself,' not by the church or the brother–all these striving to save, not to condemn him. Now, Matthew 18:18, then, and then only is that text fulfilled, having been done in accordance with the Lord's word it becomes the action of the Lord and is accepted in heaven. If a brother trespass against the church breaking the Sabbath, for instance—it is the place of the elder to restore such an one, and not for the church to rebuke openly (read Matthew 18:15–17), and the duties of an elder given in a previous lecture, going with witnesses the second time if necessary, and finally bringing it before the church, if nothing else can be done.

"Now, about speaking to only those who commit the fault. (1) When a brother has committed a fault and he is restored, remember that is to be the last of it. It is not to be told to another afterwards. The Saviour has forbidden us telling anyone but him at any time. Now, Matthew 5:22–24, so there is a check upon him also, and he cannot be at peace until he hears the brother. He must stop and go and be reconciled to his brother. Now, read Psalm 15:1–3; margin also—we are not to receive a reproach against a brother. Exodus 23:1 'shalt not receive a false report,' the Hebrew version reads. What is a false report? The telling of what we do not know, personally, to be true, even though it may be true. To repeat such a thing is the same as to tell a lie. We are not to indulge in hearsay, so no story can go beyond the one who tells it without bearing false witness, and the breaking of the ninth commandment. Leviticus 19:16. Who is a tale bearer? Read Proverbs 12:13.

"And you will always know. Never meddle with such an one; a faithful man covers it over and tries to stop its mischief. So Proverbs 20:19—'Can you keep a secret?' say they. Answer then, 'Yes, can you?' If it is a secret I have no right to confide it to any one, to betray what is told in confidence is treachery. Why do we tell one brother of his fault and he alone? Leviticus 19:17 and the margin. The same is in Matthew 18. It is done to save him from his sin, but if I refuse to go to him and he continues in his evil way, then I become partaker of his sin. Cain said 'Am I my brother's keeper?' Yes, brethren, we are helpers of one another. Now again, 'Take heed how ye hear.' It is next to impossible to listen to a statement and be able to repeat it as we hear it, It will receive the cast of each mind through which it passes, so we should heed what is said, that we have to repeat, or else we will convey a different impression from what the narrator intended. Then again, remember what was told you in a previous lecture, 'receive not an accusation against an elder,' 1 Timothy 5:19–21. And why this solemn charge—2 Peter 2:9–11? Chiefly because there are those who despise government, and speak evil dignities, and in doing this they put themselves above the angels, and become as Satan who accuses the brethren day and night. But why bring Christ in here? Read Jude 6. Well then, in doing so we put ourselves above Christ. Now, James 4:11, in doing this we start where Satan did, and that is where we will go if we continue this work."

THE CAMP MEETING

Elder A.T. Jones Leaves To Attend The Camp Meeting At Williamsport, PA.

His Last Lecture on the Evils of Religious Legislation—All Should Read it—The True Position of Dr. Crafts and other National Reformers—They Reject the Gospel of Christ and Repudiate Its Principles—Busy Times at the Camp and Many New Arrivals— Crowds on the Grounds Sunday but Fly Before the Wind Storm— The New Camp Programs.

Special Correspondence of the CAPITAL

CAMPGROUND, OTTAWA, KAN., May 20...

THERE HAS BEEN A SERIES OF HEAVY SHOWERS with sometimes hail, for a few days, attended with sunshine, which interferes somewhat with the different exercises and seriously incommodes [sic] the new comers who are pouring in. As far as classes of instruction go, this has been a busy time since the institute closed and the workers' meeting began. As many as four canvassers classes' have been in session at one and the same time, and besides three or four meetings of other kinds perhaps during the same hours. The canvassers, however, under the generalship of Captain Eldridge and his Lieutenant Belden seem to out flank the conference committee every time and get in more meetings than all the other branches of work. Every thing is bustle and activity and much good and profitable instruction is being given and received, so that cheerful faces are seen everywhere in spite of the mud and wet and even though the workers do crowd the ministers so closely that the latter are seriously pondering the question whether or no they have any "rights" at a campmeeting, yet all feel it is good to be here, and rejoice, pressing forward in harmony. Elder Jones and wife have left, he going to the campmeeting at Williamsport, Pennsylvania, and she to their home in Battle Creek, Michigan Elder Olson leaves for the latter place tomorrow, going from there to Colorado, and then to Minneapolis. Elder W.C. White and D.T. Jones will remain throughout the week, and Mrs. White will be with us to the close of the meeting. The park was crowded Sunday afternoon, but a heavy wind and rain storm scattered the people towards sundown. The following program takes the place of the one previously printed in the Capital, and will remain in force throughout the balance of the campmeeting.

CAMP PROGRAM

05:30 p.m.	Young people in west tent, foreigners in cast tent, all others in the tabernacle.
08:00 a.m.	Family Worship—Children in west tent, conference committee in office, all others in district tents.
09:00 a.m.	Annual Business meeting.
10:30 a.m.	Bible Readings—For the public and those new in the faith in the tabernacle, for older membership in the east tent, for young people in the west tent, for Bible workers and for foreigners under grand stand.
12:00 a.m.	Consultations—District leaders in west tent, reception committee in the east tent.
02:30 p.m.	The afternoon sermon or lecture.
04:30 p.m.	Annual business meetings.
06:15 p.m.	Sabbath school teachers in west tent, canvassers in the east tent.
07:30 p.m.	The evening sermon or lecture.

THE CLOSING LECTURE OF ELDER JONES

"WE WANT TO EXAMINE TONIGHT WHAT AUTHORITY THERE IS for Sunday laws. In the hearing before the senate committee, the following colloquy took place. Mr. Jones in answer to the question raised by Mr. Wood, that the conscientious convictions did not require us to work on the first day of the week, the sixth day, I wish to rend Judge Cooley's opinion.

Mr. Wood: I referred to the Bible.

Mr. Jones: Well Judge Cooley's opinion is of force in law. Judge Cooley says: "But the Jew who is forced to respect the first day of the week when his conscience requires of him the observance of the seventh also, may plausibly urge that the law discriminates against his religion, and by forcing him to keep a second Sabbath in each week, unjustly, though by indirection, punishes him for his belief." I have shown …

111

The chairman: He says "plausibly." That word "plausibly" might indicate that there are some counter views somewhere.

Mr. Jones: The argument is unanswerable. The supreme court of Pennsylvania mention certain grounds upon which this is sustained. I read further from Judge Cooley, he says:

> The laws which prohibit ordinary employment on Sunday are to be defended either on the same grounds, which justify the punishment of profanity, or as establishing sanitary regulations, based upon the demonstration of experience that one day's rest in seven is needful to recuperate the exhausted energies of body and mind.

That is the basis of this petition. This answer to that is this:

> The supreme court of Pennsylvania has preferred to such legislation on the second ground rather than the first, but it appears to us that if the benefit to the individual is alone to be considered, the argument against the law which he may make who has already observed the seventh day of the week, is unanswerable.

Stephen J. Field claimed years ago that scientists and statesmen had proven that man required one day's rest in seven for his physical system, but he did not try to show why man needed two days instead of one. All this is a fraud. It comes in with that 'one day in seven' theory, and it came in as I have already shown, in the sixteenth century through Mr. Nicholas Bowne.

Mr. Blair said: He also holds that for the general, the public good, Sunday laws are constitutional.

Mr. Jones: Yes; so as to be dispensed upon authority. Then the next sentence is as follows:

> But, on the other ground, it is clear that these laws are supportable on authority, notwithstanding the inconvenience which they occasion to those whose religious sentiments do not recognize the sacred character of the first day of the week.

That is Judge Cooley's way of answering an unanswerable argument, and that has been the way since Zosoman's time, who when asked on what authority he issued certain edicts, answered 'It has pleased the apostolic see' so in the English Parliament; they levied a tax and our fathers refused to submit, and we refuse now.

Mr. Jones: What authority is there for Sunday laws?

The chairman: That is what you have been discussing, but you seem to say that because Sunday laws are supported by authority it is the only argument in favor of a bad law, that there is authority for it. But there may be good authority for the Sunday law.

Mr. Jones: That is what is shown here, that there is no good authority for it, when it unjustly punishes a man for his unbelief.

The chairman: He does not say it is bad.

Mr. Jones: But it is. Is there any answer to an unanswerable argument?

"I want to examine tonight what authority there is for Sunday laws. Dr. Crafts, Dr. Herrick Johnson and the others claim as a basis the fourth commandment. What authority is there then in the fourth commandment for Sunday laws? Now, this is a question of legislation and of law, so then let us examine it from a legal standpoint. If the bill should pass, and become a law, the courts will be guided on its interpretation by certain well established rules, one of which is: 'What a court has to do is to declare the law as written.' Now, suppose the law takes cognizance of the fourth commandment. If they do they must take it as it is written, and it says the seventh day is the Sabbath, and this very first rule of law will shut out the Sunday law. But they will say, 'It does not say which seventh day.' Now it is plain that it is the seventh day after six days of work by the Creator at creation, and consequently it must be the seventh day of a circle of seven, and as the New Testament shows the Sabbath, is past before the first day of the week appears, read Mark 16:1–2; Luke 24:1.

"The second rule is 'In the case of all laws, it is the intent of the law giver that it is to be enforced.' Now what was the intent of the Law Giver? Was it not the seventh day that He wished to be kept? Did He not prove them all through the wilderness, by the fall of manna on six days, the double portion on the sixth day and none on the seventh for forty years? Did he not show what day he required to be kept? Well, according to law then, the courts can never uphold Sunday laws of the fourth commandment. Another rule is 'When words are plain in a written law, there is an end to all construction; they must be followed.' There is no room for construction where the words are common and such as the people can understand. How many words are there in the fourth commandment that are not plain? Not one. The words are not only plain, but the plainest, purest of English. Courts then must declare against the law, if they are going to remain courts of law, but the theologians will come in with their theological definitions and expect the courts to follow them and so turn the courts into courts of theology. But when they attempt to say that the expression is indefinite they assume authority that no man has, because if it is indefinite the Lord made it so and no power on earth can make it definite. They first declare it to be indefinite and then go about to declare it definite by putting Sunday in.

113

"If the courts go against the common rules of law another rule is violated which says:

> No forced or unnatural construction shall be put upon the language of a statute. To make the phrase 'the seventh day' in that commandment indefinite, and mean any one day in seven, and not any seventh day in particular, or to make the commandment support the observance of the first day of the week in commemoration of the resurrection, is not only to put a forced construction and a most unnatural one, upon it but is a direct violation of that other rule: 'A constitution or statute is not to be make to mean one thing at one time and another at some subsequent time when the circumstances may have so changed as perhaps to make a different rule in the case seem desirable. The meaning of the constitution (or statute) is fixed when it is adopted, and it is not different at any subsequent time when a court has occasion to pass upon it.

"I quote again from the hearing before the senate committee, from the argument of Dr. Herrick Johnson:

> Dr. Johnson: This appointment of one day in seven is arbitrary. There is nothing in nature to indicate that division of time. There is the day of twenty-four hours, there is the month and there is the year, all these are natural divisions; but there is nothing in nature to indicate the weekly division; the observance of one day in seven. It is arbitrary, and we regard that as an evidence of its Divine origin.

> The Chairman: How do you base the Sabbath itself upon the Divine ordinance when there is no natural law to indicate which day is to be observed?

> Dr. Johnson: It is in Revelation, and is found to be exactly in accord with the laws of nature.

> The Chairman: You base the law of one day's rest in seven upon Revelation' that is to say upon the Bible?

> Dr. Johnson: Yes sir.

> The Chairman: There are many who doubt that it is established by Revelation, are there not?'

> Dr. Johnson: I think no one who accepts the Bible doubts that there is one day in seven to be observed as a day of rest.

> The chairman: Will you state the authority?

> Mr. Johnson: There are references to this law all through the Bible.

114

The chairman: Now you come and change that Sabbath day to which the Lord there refers?

Mr. Johnson: That we hold was changed by the Lord Himself.

The chairman: When did He do that, and by what language?

Mr. Johnson: There was a meeting for worship on the first day in the week, the day the Lord arose, and seven days after there was another meeting for the same purpose, and then it is referred to as the Lord's day.

The chairman: After the change?

Mr. Johnson: Yes sir, after the change.

The chairman: It is based, then, upon two or three days being observed as days of religious worship, after the resurrection?

Mr. Johnson: Yes sir.

"This then, is all the authority they have for Sunday observance, and yet they go to the fourth commandment as a basis. What then is it all but going contrary to the statute? The commandment was established and adopted long before there was any need of a resurrection, and the seventh day was the meaning and intention of its Author long before such a necessity could have existed, and it cannot, therefore, be made to mean another thing now. Another rule of law is this: 'A court or legislature which should allow a change of public sentiment to influence it in giving to a written constitution a construction not warranted by the intention of its founders would be justly chargeable with reckless disregard of official oath and public duty.'

"Now what is it that these theologians ask Congress to do? Is it not to have the law give a construction to the commandments that God never intended? This is precisely what Senator Blair asks Congress to give them power to do. Senator Blair's bill refers to Sunday as 'the Lord's day.' If, then the bill had become a law, would not the courts have to search the Bible to ascertain from it what day the Lord claimed as His? In such a case, what would have been learned? The first declaration is this: 'The Son of man is Lord also of the Sabbath.' The next: 'The seventh day is the Sabbath.' Very well then, the Son of man is the Lord of the seventh day. All must admit that this conclusion is logical and cannot be successfully controverted. Hence, whatever day it is that Christ is the lord of, that day is the Sabbath. John said, 'I was in the Spirit on the Lord's day,' and therefore John was in the Spirit on the seventh day. But the argument of these men will be, 'The courts are not to set themselves up as interpreters of the Bible, but simply to decide what the law means.' In doing this what will it be? They first assert that Sunday is the Lord's day and then compel people to accept it as such whether they are willing to do so or not. There is no authority for Sunday laws in the fourth commandment, and, therefore, to obtain authority the courts of law will have to be turned into courts of theology, and the church will have to dictate to the courts, thus ruling the state.

"Now the Sunday laws of the younger states are all based upon the laws of the older ones, every one of the original thirteen states having a state religion and Sunday laws. These older ones obtained theirs from England and it from the papacy. The British system is the papal under a Christian name, and back of it all paganism from which it animated. The first Sunday, as we have seen was appointed by Constantine, who assumed the title Pontifex Maximus of the Christians and the pagan title also that in his dual capacity he might please all his subjects. A high authority asserts that the title he used, Dies Solis, is a sufficient evidence of the pagan idea (day of the sun, i.e., sun-day) that attached to its origin, and this was Constantine's idea to harmonize the different elements to the new faith. This is the only authority there is for the observance of the Sunday. There is none whatever in the Scriptures. Then instead of making efforts to establish Sunday laws, should we not aim to blot them out from our state statute books, and raise the legislation and the constitution of the states up to the level of the Constitution of the United States? It has been suggested that the next application to Congress shall be more modest than the former one, so that no attempt at religious legislation will appear in it—they will ask simply that the government employees be allowed to rest on Sunday—but it is the duty of every good citizen to oppose to the last, every attempt to legislate upon the question of Sunday laws or Sunday observance in any form. These men want to establish a precedent. If they can get the government to recognize the principle that a state has a right to legislate on these subjects, their demands will increase until finally they obtain full power by laws favoring their position entire. Dr. Crafts says of this new policy: 'It will lead to something more satisfactory.' That was Constantine's argument precisely in the fourth century, and the result was the creation of the papacy, and just so surely as Congress takes the first step, however innocent it may appear, just so sure a papacy will follow.

"Now I want to speak of the petitions that were presented to Congress, claiming to contain 14,000,000 names and show you the wickedness and dishonesty in the whole scheme, and leave it for you to decide if anything but evil can come of such unholy methods. When Senator Blair presented the petition to Congress said to contain 14,000,000 names, he made the statement that there were only 407 bona fide signatures. I wrote personally to the senator and asked if this statement was correct, and he replied that it was, and said: 'I read the extract which you find in the Record from memoranda furnished in the common way by those who requested the presentation,' and adds: 'You can have access to the files or any friend, if you can not attend to it, and get the facts as to signatures.' Foot after foot of the rolls of the petition, the names are all signed by the same hand, one hand for a foot or more in length, and another for the next, and so on. How did this come about? All but the writer's name is given by 'endorsement,' he writing all the names and attaching a certificate signed by himself that the parties endorsed the petition. These personal signatures are all the bona fide names there are. A minister would read the petition in church, and ask all to assent to it. If, say fifty, out of the 300 present perhaps signified their acquiescence he would retire to his study and under order from headquarters fill in the names of every attendant at the church, even the names of those who were not present, because, as one explained, 'silence gives consent, and we must obey orders anyway.' And now they are going over the ground again by order of the secretary of the National Reform Association who sent out a circular requesting them to obtain this time, the personal signature of each church member, and so 'duplicate' the names. When this is carried out then, and they add these new lists to the old, they will have 28,000,000 names instead of 14,000,000.

"Now as to 'endorsing' the petitions, Miss Bateham, the attorney for the W.C.T.U., says: 'Signatures are most valuable but endorsements count up fastest.' In Indianapolis, Dr. Crafts obtained the signatures of 240 Knights of Labor to the petition, and because they were delegates to a convention from other points, he claimed the whole body of Knights in the United States 'by endorsement'—240,000 in all. Again Cardinal Gibbons wrote a letter in which he said: 'I am most happy, to add my name,' and on the strength of this one signature the 7,200,000 Catholics in the United States were added to the petitions 'by endorsement.' Mr. D.E. Lindsey of Baltimore wrote to the cardinal asking if he intended, by saying his name, to include all other Catholics, and I read you his reply through his secretary:

In reply to your favor dated February 25,1889, duly received, His Eminence Cardinal Gibbons desires me to write to you that whatsoever countenance His Eminence has given to the "Sunday law" referred to in your favor, as he had not the authority, so he had not the intention, of binding the archbishops, the bishops, or the Catholic laity of the United States. His Eminence bids me say to you that he was moved to write a letter favoring the passage of the bill, mainly from a consideration of the rest and recreation which would result to our poor overworked fellow citizens, and of the facility which it would then afford them of observing the Sunday in a religious and decorous way. It is incorrect to assume that His Eminence, in the alleged words of Senator Blair, set forth in your favor, signed the bill, thus pledging 7,200,000 Catholics as endorsing the bill. I have the honor to remain, with much respect, yours faithfully,

---

[Signed] J.P. DONAHUE, Chancellor

"If it is borne in mind, also, that a large portion of these Catholics are members of the Knights of Labor, already counted, 'duplicating' comes in again. So, too the general conferences of the Methodist, Presbyterian, Baptist and Dutch Reformed churches 'endorsed' the petitions and Dr. Crafts therefore counted in all the members of these denominations, although already endorsed in their respective Churches by their pastors. Further, a large percent of the membership of the Methodist, Presbyterian and Baptist Churches are members also of the W.C.T.U., all of whom had been previously counted, thus triplicating their names, and in the new petitions it will be quadrupling them. As to the Catholic signatures, it is not true the petition finds favor among them. Catholic dignitaries and the laity all over the country are signing the remonstrance against such legislation. One gentleman in Minneapolis Minnesota, procured the signatures of over 1,200 bishops, priests, nuns, etc., and nearly every Catholic to whom the remonstrance is presented signs it. Further, in the petition presented to Congress by these men, it is claimed that every signature is that of persons 'over 21 years of age,' while, as seen above, all the Catholics of all ages had been counted, and in Sunday schools the names of all the children even infants, have been taken.

"I want to show you how Dr. Crafts succeeded in obtaining the signatures of the Knights of Labor at Indianapolis. He was asked if it would be best for the government to control all the railroads and to stop Sunday trains. He replied, 'I believe in that,' and said, in substance, 'if the railroads refuse what we now ask, the people may demand control over all the work.' He then read the following petition, the same as is being extensively circulated now in Minnesota and other states: 'Petition of adult citizens of the state of –for a six-day law. To the state senate: The undersigned earnestly petition your honorable body to pass a bill forbidding anyone to hire another or to be hired for more than six days of any week, except in domestic service and the care of the sick, in order that those whom law or custom permits to work on Sunday may be protected in their right to some other weekly rest day, and in their right to a week's wages for six day's work.'

"No wonder he obtained their signatures, yet there are many knights who could not be induced to sign any petitions favoring Sunday legislation, in any form. The principle underlying the above quoted petition is genuine socialism. If a man can legally collect pay for a day more than he works, he can demand pay for not working at all. If he is entitled to seven days' pay for six day's labor, then six days' pay can be demanded for five days' work, five days' for four, four days' for three, three days' for two, two days' for one, and one day for no work at all. Is not this the logical sequence? But it may be claimed that these men do not really mean to demand seven days' pay for six days' labor, but I can show you that they do. In Reverend George Elliott's argument before the senate committee the following questions from Senator Call and answered by Mr. Elliott appear:

> Senator Call: Do you propose that Congress shall make provision to pay the people in the employ of the government who are exempted on Sunday for Sunday work?

Mr. Elliott: I expect you to give them an adequate compensation.

Senator Call: Do you propose that the law shall provide that the same amount shall be paid for six days' work as for seven?

Mr. Elliott: I do, for the reason that we believe these employees can do all the work that is to be done in six days, and if they do all the work they ought to have all the pay.

Let us pause here and ask the working man seriously this question. If these men succeed in their effort to 'rescue' you from the 'monopolies' that oppress you, who will afterwards rescue you from the religious monopoly into which they seek to drag you? And bear in mind that a religious monopoly is the most terrible and formidable of any the earth has ever seen. My friends, when ministers go about on such business as this, deliberately pandering to the socialistic tendencies of the laboring classes and truckling to the dogma of the Catholic church, that the priests have a right to dictate to the people how they shall act and speak, carrying this principle into their own churches, even boasting that they control certain numbers of votes which they are willing to trade off for political favors. When ministers go about on such business they are everything but ministers of the gospel. And that the gospel will be, nay has been, rejected in the prosecution of their nefarious schemes, I will show you. There was held in Columbus, Ohio, last February what was called the Ohio International Sabbath convention, held in the interests of Sunday legislation, and was supposed to represent the entire denominations in the state. A large number of prominent speakers were present including Dr. Wilbur F. Crafts and Hon. Thomas McDougall of Cincinnati who had been specially invited. I want to show you that this gentleman presented the gospel of Jesus Christ as the proper means of regenerating mankind, and that this convention (having among it vice president and others of the National Reform Association) deliberately rejected the gospel and refused to allow the gentleman to speak again. I make extracts from the speech which can be found printed in full in the American Sentinel, Oakland, California, issue of April 3. 'Being in full sympathy with every well directed and reasonable movement for a better observance of the civil Sabbath, I respond to your call on me to speak. The evils existing and complained of are in our large cities (speaking of the indulgence etc.). How is existing law to be enforced in them? Their welfare is the problem of the statesman and the Christian.

"Any law on this subject which depends for its enforcement on a resort to a jury, in the existing state of public sentiment in our large cities, must be of necessity a failure under any fair system of selecting a jury which represents the community from which it is drawn. What, then is to be done? Seek the highest good attainable. The redemption of the masses in our large cities and their elevation to a better observance of law is to be sought through the gospel of Jesus Christ. Ministering in His name, go to their homes, seek their welfare, educate them by the power and teaching of Jesus Christ, and there will come to you that reform you seek. They are waiting for His service, His education. Not in conventions; not in resolutions; not in the fiats of legislation, but give your time, money, prayer, and service to carrying to the homes of the toiling masses the beneficent gospel, and you will elevate and reform, as nothing else can do or will, those whom you now regard as the enemies of the Sabbath. Let us learn that this is an intensely practical question, presenting questions for our consideration difficult to solve and which no legislation can solve. The roots of the evil are deeper; they need the gospel of Christ as the power to give us what we desire. Abandon agitation and service for the unattainable and consecrate your time, money, prayers and service to carrying to those for whom Christ died, His gospel of love and His ministry of service.' In the very next meeting after this address, a motion was made 'that this convention is not in accord with Mr. McDougall's speech.' The motion was carried unanimously and without debate. A similar meeting had been arranged in Cincinnati for the following Saturday for Mr. McDougall to speak, but when the committee read his Columbus speech they waited upon the gentleman and asked him if the speech he made at Columbus embodied the sentiments he expected to express at Cincinnati. Upon receiving his reply that it did, they requested him not to attend the meeting, and as Mr. McDougall replied that he was not in the habit of 'going where he was not wanted—'the speaker of the meeting'—was not present. Now then, in repudiating the doctrine of Jesus Christ, are these men not logically consistent? Certainly they are, because if they can make men righteous by legislation what need have they for the gospel? Further, can these political ministers be followers of the meek and lowly Jesus, who repudiated politics, and said 'My kingdom is not of this earth.' The gospel of Christ does not consort well with political scheming; and suggestions to preach the Gospel and to work by gospel methods and means are not palatable to the political preacher.

"Under our constitution and government this country has been the example to all the world. Its example has carried forward all nations into a broader light. Is not this a grand testimony in favor of our constitution and country as it now is? When then, those men attempt to alter the religious and civil freedom which we now enjoy, and which has been such a regenerating power, by its example on other nations, and seek to substitute for it enforcement of religious legislation and religious intolerance, relegating the nation back into the dark ages again, what will be the consequences to other countries? Why they will degenerate backward also, the papacy will again rear its head and become supreme, and a living image of it be set up in our own country upon a papal basis."

THE CAMP MEETING

The General Meeting And
First Session Of Conference

Full Report of the Conference Proceedings—Committees
Appointed—Tract and Missionary Society Proceedings—Report of
the Treasurer–New Arrivals Crowd the Dining Room—Hot Soup
and "Crust" Coffee in the Early Mornings.

Special Correspondence of the CAPITAL

CAMP MEETING, OTTAWA, KAN. May 22...

THE ANNUAL CONFERENCE OF SEVENTH-DAY ADVENTISTS for the state of Kansas
convened at 9 o'clock a.m. Tuesday, May 21, this being the fifteenth annual
convention. The president, C.A. Hull, called the brethren to order, and was
followed by prayer by Elder O. A. Olson, president of the general conference,
Elder W.C. White also being present. By order, the minutes of the last conference were read by the secretary, L. J. Rousseau, when Elder C. C. Reynolds
called attention to the error in change of the name of the church, it being
Altoona instead of Chanute, after which the minutes were approved. The secretary then read the names of the delegates who had handed in credentials,
which (besides the ordained ministers, Elders John Gibbs, S.S. Shrock, Joseph
LaMont, Smith Sharp, C. C. McReynolds, W. W. Stebbins, L. T. Rousseau, M.
H. Gregory and C. P. Haskell), were the following: Alton, M. E. McReynolds,
Centerville, S. N. Ayers; Caney, E. T. Burch; Dennis, T. M. Thom; Deer Creek,
0. S. Ferrin; Emporia, Fannie Cook, M. Moore, C. A. Haas; Felsburg, William
Jared; Fort Scott, O. S. Hullingsworth; Greerdeaf, O. Mathleson; Hutchinson,
J. M. Jones, H. P. Baker, M. A. Patton; Lone Elm, Rufus Baker; Louisville,
H. N. Copeland; Moline, J. M. Gibbs; Newton, W. W. Stebbins; Ottawa, J. L.
Bellbart, A. E. Field, P. P. Wilcox, S. C. Osbome; Oronoque, J. H. Rogers; Poret,
Nettie Dixon, N. P. Dixon; Rotate, Lizzie Farnsworth; Stover, N. W. Vincent;
Savery, Sarah Atiken, Robert Atiken; Topeka, Howard Parsons, L. Winston,
E. F. Detter, L. Dye Chambers, George Night, George W. Eddy; Valley Center,

I. S. Welch, T. R. Owing, Valeda; E. R. Carpenter, R. H. Miller; Wichits, J. H. Baker, Bell Fend, John R. Ogden; El Dorado, Elizabeth Pirtle, Mollie Pirtle; Harvey County, W. J. Jacob; Otis, John Mason, G. H. Mohr, John Smidt.

It was moved that the ministerial brethren from abroad be invited to take part in the proceedings.

THE WEEK OF PRAYER

THE WEEK OF PRAYER WAS UNIVERSALLY OBSERVED and resulted in great good, the spiritual tone of the churches was improved. God seemed to come near to the people, and the season of devotion was felt to be profitable and elevating.

WORK WITH THE PETITIONS

THE BRETHREN GENERALLY TOOK UP THE MATTER ENERGETICALLY and circulated them freely. The entire canvassing force devoted one week to this duty exclusively, one company, that in Leavenworth, laid aside their canvassing and engaged in presenting their petitions for signatures for three weeks, resulting in procuring over 4,000 signatures. The daily papers did not a first understand their work and some opposed it violently, but the canvassers interviewed the editors, explained their position and the situation changed completely, the papers not only taking their stand with us, but commending our canvassers warmly and recommending and endorsing their work. The petitions were carried around before the canvassing began and did not affect the latter. As a result of the efforts with the petitions over 26,000 names have been sent in from these protesting against religious legislation, and there are now on hand over 1,000 more to be sent off.

THE SCHOOL

THIS IS A SUBJECT THAT HAS BEEN TALKED OVER CONSIDERABLY for some years and the interest in the matter seemed to increase from year to year until a trial school was started this year at Ottawa, using the church building. Seats, stoves, etc., needed were purchased and Elder L. J. Rousseau and wife installed as teachers. Some thirty-five pupils attended, the brethren of the Ottawa church boarding them. The donations of $300 for a sinking fund and the tuition fee about paid all the expenses, and so in every way, except the attendance, the school met all the expectations of the conference committee.

"In reference to the work in New Mexico I can not do better," the president said, "than to read the following resolution:

WHEREAS, New Mexico is more closely connected with Colorado than with Kansas, and the Colorado conference is willing to take that field and carry out the proposition

122

made to the Kansas conference, therefore resolved, that the Kansas Conference release all claims on New Mexico, and on the tent offered by the General Conference, and on the fund raised in Kansas to be used in opening up the work in New Mexico, in favor of the Colorado conference, except so much of the fund raised as has already been expended on canvassers out to that field.

SUGGESTIONS BY THE PRESIDENT

THE FOLLOWING SUGGESTIONS WERE MADE by the president. That the work at Leavenworth be given a tent and corps of teachers.

That a good tract, and missionary man be sent into the field, and that Brother L. Dye Chambers be sent out in the interests of this work.

That someone el se should be sent out in the interests of Sabbath school work.

On motion the usual committees were announced.

Auditing—L. Winston, T. J. Eagle, J. H. Baker, E. M. Gwin, J. D. Rockey.

On Nominations—L Winston, John Gibbs, R. Dobbins, T. J. Eagle, O. S. Ferrew.

On Resolutions—R. C. Porter, James Merrow, W. W. Stebbins.

On Licenses and Credentials—D. T. Jones, C. McReynolds, L. Dye Chambers, E. H. Gates, Genesis Jennings.

On Auditing Treasurer's Book—J. Lamont, J. S. Thup.

The matter of the school and the school committee requiring a separate motion it was moved seconded and carried that the matter receive immediate attention. The president made the following nominations. School committee: T. J. Eagle, L. J. Rousseau, John Helitgae, L. Winston, L. Dall, A. G. Miller.

THE TRACT AND MISSIONARY SOCIETY

THE MEETING WAS OPENED BY PRESIDENT HALL, after which the record of the last year's proceedings at Emporia, Kan., was read by the secretary, L. Dye Chambers, and was approved. The secretary then read the financial statement for the last year. In the course of the reading the secretary called attention to the fact that the brethren and sisters loan the Society from time to time sums of money they have on hand idle, and that this course had greatly assisted the work, and then asked for sums from others and that they be sent with a statement of how long they can remain. If a definite date is named, the money will be returned promptly on the specified day. If no definite date can be given, send a week or two weeks' notice before ordering its return.

The increase of $3,088.04 is due almost entirely to increase work on the part of the canvassers, because work done by ministers and the brethren fell behind over $700 this year, or over one-third behind that of last year. The balance in favor of the Society of $3,696.21 supposes all accounts and notes on hand as good for their face value, and although the statement shows an apparent increase in valuation during the year of $316.26, yet there are bad debts contracted that will overbalance this increase. The secretary called attention to the decrease of individual work performed by the members occasioning a loss of over $700, and urged increased effort. The details of his report showed also that the debts from local societies are enlarging which ought not to be so, and pleaded that an effort be made to decrease this indebtedness. In speaking of the canvassers' work, he said that this year the sales were $415,748.40, against a little over $8,000 last year, owing to the increase in number of the canvassers, and extra value of the books canvassed for. A detailed statement was given of this which we have no space to present. Of *Bible Readings* alone over 1,500 copies were sold, the total of 8,617 books being a good record; yet it had been done at a loss to the Society; many of the canvassers being too poor to pay their way have run in debt to the Society fully $1,500 in the last two to five years, being a class of debts not easily, if ever paid, and which cripples the Society in its work. The original capital in 1884 was $4,255.88 and this year it is $17,162.76—an increase of $12,903.88—nearly four times as much then, notwithstanding there has been no increase of capital but a constant drain. Such a condition necessitates a heavy debt at the *Review* office, and while the stock on hand is larger than last year, yet our debts increase it too great a ratio, because our capital has become too small for the business we have to attend to, hence grows to large proportions. He urged the payment of unpaid pledges. If this was done the debt would be decreased over one half. There are other brethren who are able to put money in this work, and an appeal was made to such to come forward and aid the Society by their means.

REPORT OF THE SECRETARY AND TREASURER

[condensed]

Cash receipts during the year $16,162.96

Cash receipts during the last year $13,074.92

Increase during the year .... $ 3,088.04

FINANCIAL STANDING OF THE SOCIETY

Total assets $10,621.63

Total liabilities .... $ 6,925.42

Balance in favor of the Society .... $ 3,696.21

Balance in favor of the Society last year .... $ 3,379.85

Increase in valuation during year .... $ 316.36

REPORT OF AUDITING COMMITTEE,
TOPEKA, KAN., April 22

We, your committee, appointed to invoice the stock and audit the books of the treasurer of the Kansas Tract and Missionary Society, find:

Stock on hand to the value of .... $ 3,799.07

Furniture and fixtures .... $ 244.20

Cash on hand .... $ 648.99

Due from districts .... $ 1,355.78

Due from individuals .... $ 468.59

Total assets $10,621.63

Total liabilities .... $ 6,925.42

Net assets .... $ 3,696.21

and find the books correctly kept.

T.D. Rockey, J. LaMont, Smith Sharp .... Committee.

Total number subscription booklets sold, 8,617; total price, $15,748.40.

A motion was then made and carried to appoint the usual committees, and the president announced the following:

On nominations: John Gibbs, J. H. Rogers, Rufus Baker, R. Dobbins, and W.W. Stebbins.

On resolutions: J. LaMont, C.P. Haskell, and E.W. Rice

Auditing: J.D. Rockey, Smith Sharp, and J. LaMont

On motion the meeting adjourned to Thursday at 4:30 p.m.

THE CAMP MEETING

Elder Porter Leaves for Sedalia— Arrival of C.A. Johnson of Nebraska

The Camp a Bee Hive of Activity, Pitching Tents, Hearing Lectures, Attending Classes of Instruction, Conference Meetings or Hunting up Sleeping Places.

Special Correspondence of the CAPITAL

CAMP MEETING, OTTAWA, KAN., May 23...

WE ARE HAVING GLORIOUS WEATHER and all is bustle and life at the camp. It is not possible to learn the total number present, every train bringing new ones, and many coming by teams , but it is safe to say that there are over 600, probably 700 now on the grounds. Every possible effort is being made by President Hail and the reception committee to care for the new arrivals, but it is a task that only they can appreciate. A room in one of the cottages has ten occupants and every available place is being utilized. So many classes of instruction also are going on at once that even the grand stand is brought into service and a Bible class meets above on the seats, and another for foreigners below, while at the same time classes and meetings of various kinds are being given and held in every tent and the tabernacle. Mr. Belden closes his labor here today and leaves for the Williamsport, Pennsylvania, camp. The Sabbath school and the H. & T. associations met yesterday. The proceedings will be found below, also a synopsis of Mrs. White's sermon. The conference work is progressing and it is expected that committees will be able to make reports promptly. Elder R. C. Porter left today to attend the convention of national reformers at Sedalia, Missouri, and Elder Johnson arrived on the evening train from Nebraska.

THE GIFTS AND CALLING OF GOD

BY E.G. WHITE

"ROMANS 2:4—Without whose repentance? Ours. This is what I wish to show you today. First as to the gifts of God–Acts 14:15–17–when the people of Lystra were about to worship Paul and Barnabas they uttered this explanation, in which is shown that when God suffered all nations to walk in their own ways, He gave them still the natural gifts without repentance. And so in Matthew 5:45, all these then come upon all, repentant and unrepentant. Now as to spiritual gifts these, too, are without repentance, John 3:16. Was this after the annual repental or before? Romans 5:6, 8, 10; Christ died then for the ungodly, for sinners and for his enemies, and in God gave everything, Romans 8:32. It does not say 'how shall He,' but 'how shall He not freely give us all things.' If He gave His own Son for sinners how can He keep from giving us all things; so in the first great gift we have everything that God can give. With Him not without Him. If we do not accept Him we cannot have the other gift but those who have Him, have all, Colossians 2:9–10. So it is true that the gifts are without repenting. Then the calling; how extensive is this? Isaiah 30:18, the calling then is unto salvation. 2 Peter 3:9 he calls to repentance. So the gifts and calling of God are without repentance. Romans 10:11–1 7. So that gift by which men call upon God is a gift of itself. God sends men to call men to Him. Acts 2:39. Where then does repentance come in? We cannot unless we repent, but Romans 2:4, last part, that is where repentance comes in. In these gifts God displays his goodness and expects the viewing of His goodness will lead men to turn to Him. Romans 10:8–10. 'If I be lifted up,' the Saviour says, 'I will draw all men to Me.' The lifting up of the Saviour was a manifestation of God's goodness. Now, Acts 5:30, 31, He is exalted to give repentance to man, so by God's goodness, is in this way, repentance is made a gift also. Now I want to read, all through the Scriptures, several texts to show this is the description He has given of Himself. Exodus 33:13; 34:5–9, shows where and when the Lord proclaimed Himself—so great, so grand, so good was God that Moses pleaded that he and the children of Israel might have a character like Him. The very purpose of all this was that men might be led from their evil to His goodness. Hosea 11:2–9; 8:12. Now, in giving the law what was it for? Because He loved men. Deuteronomy 33:2,3, Exodus 20:20.

"After He had spoken the law Moses spoke this that men might see their sins and turn to God and have their sins taken away. Now, Hosea 11:1–9, again, when the people had sinned so fearfully God represents Himself as taking them by the arm and drawing them from their evil, and even when the time came that they ought to be given up He exclaims, 'How shall I give thee up', showing his great love for them, holding back a little longer, Jeremiah 39:1. Because of the inevitable outcome of their wickedness, God was constantly trying to draw them away from the evil ways they followed. Now the New Testament, Titus 3:3–7. What made us better than we were? The love of God, our Saviour, appeared, not by our own works, but according to His disposition to trust us better than we deserve. So the tenor of the whole Scripture is that God's love draws men to repentance, all His gifts being given without it. Ephesians 2:1–2. What makes us different? 'God, who is rich in mercy for His great love wherewith He loved us, even when we were dead in sin, hath quickened us together with Christ (by grace ye are saved) and hath raised us up together and made us sit together in heavenly places in Christ Jesus, that in the ages to come He might show the exceeding riches of His grace in His kindness towards us through Jesus Christ, for by grace are ye saved, through faith, and that not of yourselves, it is the gift of God.' It is God's love, who is rich in mercy, that changed us and made us different from what we were. It is the goodness of God alone that can change us. Only by beholding it and worshipping Him can we become better as the man changes into that which he worships, being conformed into the character he worships. Read the Saviour's words in Matthew 7:10–11; Romans 3:8–19. To become better, then, we must have true and exalted views of God that we can worship Him for what He is, and so grow into His likeness. So then when He draws us to Him, He bestows upon us His goodness for His Son's sake. Is this not so? Read John 1:12 and the margin. To as many as received Him He gave them the right and privilege to become sons, with no preference, and heirs of all things—John 8:31–36—the bond servant of sin abideth not, but the Son abideth forever, that is the promise, free from sin and free indeed.

"Hebrews 2:14–15. Why in fear of death? Romans 6:21. All having sinned death waits for all and so all wait in fear, but the Saviour suffered death to deliver us by conquering Satan who had the power of death. Romans 8:1–8,17. If some then heirs of God and joint heirs with Jesus, and He is heir of all, and so all will be ours. In receiving Jesus we receive all, and it is the goodness of God that does it all. Now we receive the spirit of adoption (the bond servant not abiding in the house forever) but the spirit of adoption making us sons, Galatians 4:4–7, and this is what the Saviour said in John 8. Eternal life then belongs to such–but there is something more yet. When we receive Jesus Christ and become sons of God, then the Father loves us equally with His own Son. We all ought to know this and try to realize it, and know that God is love. Read John 17:17–23, and always remember it. God wants us to know and believe it, even if we cannot understand it. We cannot comprehend it but we can believe it, and enjoy it, and we will have all eternity to study it all. What is then our privilege to be loved, as He loves His own Son, for God is love and he that dwelleth in God dwells in love. John 17:26. What then is it that makes us good? What else but the goodness of God. Remember what John says, I John 3:1–3; It was the wonderful love that astonished him. He could only wonder and admire without understanding it. Is it not so then that the gifts and calling of God are without repentance."

THE SABBATH SCHOOL ASSOCIATION

THE TWELFTH ANNUAL SESSION OF THIS ASSOCIATION convened at 9 o'clock on Wednesday. Elder L.D. Rousseau, president in the chair. The proceedings of the last convention at Emperia were read and approved, and after brief remarks by the president, the following committees were on motion appointed:

On nominations, C. McReynolds, William Dail and C.T. Ferrin. On resolutions, W.H. Greghory, W.S. Hyett and James A. Morrow. Auditing, Ed Dexter, and John Ashcroft.

THE PRESIDENT'S ADDRESS

"I WISH TO CALL YOUR ATTENTION TO THE FACT that because of a lack of knowledge of the plans and details of Sabbath school work there is much irregularity in methods and confusion in instruction given. If a plan could be formulated, and some competent person set apart to present it to the Sabbath school and all the other ministers should be guided by the instruction of this one, as far as related to this work, all schools, members and officers would be working intelligently and in harmony with the state and international associations. I would recommend that every school in the state be visited at least once a year and be given a course of practical instruction in Sabbath school methods and work, especially the kindergarten work. Also that the kindergarten be established in every school where it is possible to introduce it, and that competent persons be selected for teachers and thoroughly instructed in what will be required of them. I also recommend that plans be made to have next year, at our annual campmeeting, a representative of the International Sabbath School Association who will come prepared to give instruction in Sabbath school work

"I also recommend that arrangements be made by which every tent company can have a series of lessons on denominational truths for adults (the young being provided for in the *Instructor*) to consist of at least twenty or twenty-five lessons."

THE HEALTH AND TEMPERANCE MEETING

The first meeting of this association was called to order by the president Dr. R. Dobbins, who stated that the secretary and treasurer being absent, it would be necessary to elect a secretary pro tem, and Mrs. Eddy was chosen. She read the minutes of the last meeting at Emporia, which were approved.

The financial report of the secretary was read and then came...

THE PRESIDENT'S ADDRESS

"I CALL YOUR ATTENTION TO THE FACT that the secretary's report covers only the financial matters relating to the health and temperance work and therefore I will briefly outline the work aside from this that has been accomplished in the past year.

"I began the work in June at Topeka where the first local Health and Temperance club was formed. During the year I visited many of our churches and delivered some ninety discourses, resulting in the enrollment of 340 members and the organization of five local clubs. Much of the labor, however, was performed at the fall camp meetings, where a large number signed the teetotal pledges who may be called members at large. Wherever I have been I have found the brethren anxious to hear and learn all that they could about hygiene and temperate living. I find the domain to be a vast one, because their subjects enter into what constitutes right living, right dressing, proper care of our bodies and social purity, in fact it is all something like John the Baptist—a forerunner. The Spirit of Prophecy declares it to be the forearm of the message, yet I am sorry to say many of our churches are far behind in a true knowledge of health laws. I find few have been taught how to bring their appetites into subjection to natural laws which are the laws of God."

In concluding he suggested the following, that the ministers give more attention to these subjects in presenting the message, because if an intelligent comprehension of the laws of health and temperance is gained previous to the acceptance of the truth, very little trouble is afterward experienced in inducing the parties to live temperately. If they are taught how and what to eat, how to dress and care for their bodies, it makes them more appreciative of the third angel's message when it is presented. He also called attention to the fact that in the general organization there is no provision made for a state society being now supported by voluntary contributions. He asked for resolutions upon that matter, yet remarked it might be necessary to go further back to the general organization.

On motion, the chair then appointed the committees. On nomination–J.H. Raker and E.E. Pitcher.

On resolutions—J. LaMont, B.P. Stebbins and J.H. Rogers.

Invitation being extended for remarks, Elder B.P. Stebbins spoke very interestingly at some length, giving personal experiences, and among other good things, he said that the people should first be converted to health and temperance, afterwards to the cause; because if one is intemperate, one cannot serve the Father acceptably, and being temperate means more than merely abstaining from the use of alcohol, tobacco, tea and coffee. If we violate nature's laws our minds as well as bodies suffer and are weak, not what God would have them to be. We cannot expect to willfully live intemperate, unhealthful lives and serve the Lord acceptably. If we were thoroughly temperate We would not see the sickness and suffering among us that is visible on every hand.

Adjourned to Sunday at 9 a.m.

THE CAMP MEETING

COMMITTEE REPORT ON THE PROPOSITION FOR A SCHOOL

Friday Devoted Almost Entirely to Conference Work–The Whole
Camp Unite in a Special Meeting at Sundown–Proceedings of the
Sabbath School Association and Names of the Newly Licensed
Brethren of the Conference.

Special Correspondence of the CAPITAL.

CAMP MEETING GROUNDS, OTTAWA, KAN., MAY 25...

T HE ENTIRE MORNING, from 9 to nearly 1 o'clock, Friday, was devoted to
conference work. In the afternoon the Sabbath School Association held
another session and elected officers for the ensuing year. The committee
on credentials and licenses for the conference also reported. The full list
of names will be found below. The committee on the proposition to erect a
school building reported. It is not definitely decided whether to build one
centrally located for all the conferences west of the Mississippi or one in
Kansas for the benefit of Colorado, Kansas, Missouri, Arkansas and Texas.
The estimates of the cost vary from $10,000 to $40,000, according to the
location and purpose. I send full reports of all the proceedings and discus-
sions. At sundown the whole camp came together for worship, as is the
custom at the beginning of the Sabbath, and the exercises were turned into
a social meeting. Over a thousand people were present, many citizens of
Ottawa having come out to listen to Mrs. White's exhortation.

THIRD SESSION OF THE ANNUAL CONFERENCE

Meeting called to order by the president, prayer by Elder Johnson,
after which the minutes of the last meeting were read and approved. On
recommendation of the president the resolutions were laid upon the table,
and the committee on credentials and requests for admission of churches

132

reported a recommendation that the following churches be admitted: Florence, Winfield, Moline, Harvey County, Grenola, Olney.

The school committee reported the following, the resolution being presented by Professor W. W. Prescott:

WHEREAS, It is evident that when a proper degree of interest is taken in the subject of education of the youth among us, Battle Creek College will not be able to meet the demands upon it and that further facilities in this direction will be required, and

WHEREAS, The expense attending the establishment and maintenance of a good school in each conference is such as to make the burden quite heavy when borne alone, and

WHEREAS, There is at present a difficulty experienced in securing suitable teachers and managers for separate conference schools therefore
Resolved,

1. That we recommend that the several conferences of the Southwest, viz.: Colorado, Kansas, Missouri, Arkansas, and Texas unite their interests on this question and establish and maintain one well equipped and centrally located school.
2. That an organization be formed, to be known as the _____ Educational Society of Seventh-day Adventists, which shall, through a board of trustees, have control of the school.
3. That the capital stock of this organization not be less than $20,000.
4. That the capital stock be divided into shares of $10 each.
5. That Kansas raise $10,000 towards the capital stock, and that the remaining $10,000 be equitably divided among the other conferences named.
6. That each of these conferences appoint, at its earliest convenience, a committee of two, as a part of a general committee, to carry these plans into effect.

The report being accepted, Professor W. W. Prescott spoke at length in favor of the resolutions. He showed the two main difficulties to the raising of the money and supplying competent teachers, yet there is a growing demand from year to year for a properly equipped and conducted school. A poor school is a poor investment. As to a conference school, opinion is divided. In the Northwest it is proposed to have one to accommodate several conferences by being centrally located. "You in Kansas know better than I the difficulties, but that there is a need of such a school I believe, yet plans must be devised to spread the burden as much as possible, and care must be taken not to enter into it in a way that may result in failure. If the conferences adjoining unite their forces so that reasonable support be given, then a success may be assured from the start. I advise no hasty action, but that when it is entered into it may be done with a determination to back it up."

The resolution being open for discussion, Dr. Landis from Lone Elm called attention to the offer of $1,000 from a citizen of his section and the possibility of others should that point be favorably considered.

Elder I.S. Schrock spoke at some length assuring the brethren of the hearty support and cooperation of the Germans if they can be assured of a German class in the school.

Elder McReynolds and others spoke briefly in favor of the school, and the suggestion was made that a committee be appointed to canvass our people in regard to raising the necessary amount. Elder Desler asked what was known of the desire of neighboring conferences to cooperate. Elder Gates of Colorado, said he did not know what the brethren might do in his conference, but he knew they were desirous of such a school and he believed they would endorse it heartily.

Elder D. T. Jones of Missouri, favored the cooperation plan and endorsed the project, but was not prepared to speak definitely for his state, yet believed it would take hold and do its part. "It is impossible," he said, "for the Battle Creek College to accept all the scholars offered, and branch schools are a necessity." Elder Hyatt of Texas, heartily endorsed the resolutions, personally, and said that his people were strongly in favor of a school of this kind, but he could not speak for the brethren of the state being, as yet a comparative stranger among them. The query was again raised as to whether it was best to ascertain if the other conferences will cooperate, and that therefore was not better to make a beginning and then add to it, as other conferences cooperate. Elder McReynolds asked if it would be necessary to wait for other conferences to convene before taking action. Mrs. White said she knew the brethren in Kansas would naturally desire the school located in Kansas, "but leave that question out for the present. Can you not vote to raise the amount necessary independent of the convention? There is poverty in Kansas and elsewhere but you will find that when the time comes, there will be those who can put means into the work. It is easier to get the buildings erected than it is to obtain the consecrated ability to run the schools after they are built. "The lady illustrated at length the reasons why the ability should be consecrated that the moral tone of the school should be kept up to the proper standard, and said that this was the great difficulty in having many schools. It is the moral and religious influence that should predominate. Our schools should be missionary fields, the effort in and out of meetings, the order of the house, all should tend to keep up the religious feeling. The question, then, to consider is whether you are willing to unite and consecrate your means and available ability to have one good school, and make that one as near perfection as possible."

Elder Sharp said there had been three propositions before the brethren: a conference school, to cost about $10,000; another by the unity of adjoining conferences to cost about $20,000 and a third, a single school east of the

Rocky Mountains and west of the Mississippi, to cost $40,000. It seems as though neither of these propositions met the want.

Mrs. White said that in connection with the schools for larger scholars it had been shown her that there should be small church schools where the little children could be taught, and that teachers from the Battle Creek College should be trained to teach in these schools.

After a recess of half an hour the meeting was called to order, and after prayer by Professor Prescott, this gentleman suggested in reference to the small church schools that the larger schools should be used to prepare and fit the sisters to go out among the churches and take charge of the small children in those schools. He then asked which the brethren thought it best to have, two schools west of the Mississippi or one centrally located. Considerable discussion followed, the majority of the feeling seeming to be in favor of the two schools, as giving the benefit to the greatest number. Professor Prescott said it must be understood that he had no plan to push through, "but the question was whether you could take the burden of two schools, and whether the properly consecrated talent could be obtained for two."

Mrs. White said she had some experience in this from the opening of the college at Battle Creek and South Lancaster and how difficult it was to procure the proper help. Now as to the financial part, "no school we have ever started has sustained itself at the start there always being a deficiency at the end of the year.

"The amount of planning and labor expended in raising the Battle Creek College to its present high standard, I am well acquainted with. Our schools do not receive any larger donations or endorsements than do others, and if you try to establish two schools it will be a great burden and not as desirable as to have one will equipped and properly managed. Now the point to consider is, where are your helps and facilities. You do not realize what it is to keep up the high standard in both religion and science. Unless you have sanctified ability you will find you have a great work on your hands."

Elder Sharp said that aside from local interests one school is preferable. The solution of this problem of education is in the church schools. There would be no necessity for another school for large pupils if it were not for that no greater numbers can be accommodated at Battle Creek. If one was established in Kansas at a cost of $10,000, it would not be as efficient as one larger central one; and further, the great question is obtaining the proper help to carry on two schools. He thought one school, centrally located, would, in the long run, be the most satisfactory. Professor Prescott said he could each year give certificates conscientiously to enough to become teachers, as competent, but the object on having schools of our own is that their religious training should be a prominent feature and in this but few could be sent out whom he could safely recommend. "This is what we mean in saying it will be difficult to obtain help to sustain many schools. Both South Lancaster and Minneapolis took from the faculty of the Battle Creek College to carry on the schools there, now where else can your help come from if you start schools? The Northwest has already voted on this question to unite and look to Battle Creek for help, and if you do the same, I do not know where the help is coming from. I want to do the best that can be done, but not do anything rashly." It seemed to be the general impression in the talks that followed that there was not help sufficient outside of Battle Creek to establish two other schools. The subject was then laid on the table to be made a special order for Saturday night. The committee on credentials reported the following: The committee on investigation finds the Louisville church entitled to three delegates, and recommend that R. Dobbins and Sarah Brink act as delegates in addition to the one already represented. Also at a meeting of said church a request was made to the conference in session to change the name of the church from Louisville to Wamego, and your committee sees no reason why their request should not be granted. We also recommend the names of A. S. Combs and H. C. Fitzgerald as delegates from Neosho Rapids Church, and George Jennings as delegate from the Pittsburgh church. Also that the name of Clark Township Church be changed to Tampa. W. H. Sugery, chairman of committee. Carried.

The committee on license and credentials made the following partial report: For credentials: C. McReynolds, C. P. Haskell, M. H. Gregory, J. LaMont, Smith Sharp, W. W. Stebbens, L. J. Rousseau, John Gibbs.

For license: C. A. Hali, E. Loeppke, A. A. Maier, N. W. Vincent, E. S. Fortner, J. S. Thorp, T. U. Thom, E. P. Dexter, J. S. Beilbart.

For missionary license: N. P. Dixon and Rufus Baker.

That G. T. Haffner engage in the canvassing work as long as directed to do so by the conference committee.

That N. Drake is recommended to go to school at Battle Creek, and canvass in the interval. [Signed by the full committee.] Report adopted.

Elder D. T. Jones offered the following resolution, which was adopted:

WHEREAS, God has blessed us with light of the third angel's message, and has laid upon us the responsibility of sending it to the world; and

WHEREAS, There is an urgent necessity for means to support our foreign missions that are already established, and establish and maintain missions in other foreign countries, therefore

Resolved, That we as a conference endorse the plan of first day offerings as recommended by the General Conference, and that we will use our influence as individuals to have all our people lay by on the first day of the week for the support of foreign missions. Elder Jones spoke at length on the resolutions, giving many interesting facts and figures to show what the result would be if these offerings were made systematic and continuous, and that if the plan is generally adopted there will be no lack of funds. A gratuitous tract on the subject of foreign missions can be procured, he said, from the *Review* office, Battle Creek, Michigan Mrs. White gave a very interesting account of her lengthy stay among the foreign missions; of the condition and spread of the work abroad; the expense attending the prosecution of the word; sketches of workers, their experiences and trials. Adjourned

THE CAMP MEETING

The Great Gathering
A Thing Of The Past

The Sabbath School on Saturday–Professor W.W. Prescott's
Sermon–The Action of the Conference in Reference to the School
Still In Doubt–The Majority in Favor of Kansas as the Location.

Special Correspondence of the CAPITAL

CAMPMEETING, OTTAWA, KAN., May 27...

THE SABBATH (SATURDAY) DAWNED CLEAR and sunshiny, though cold. At 9 o'clock the great gathering of the day took place in the tabernacle, the Sabbath school. There were 108 classes in all–2 Scandinavian, 9 German, 5 kindergarten, 7 primary, 8 intermediate and 67 senior–with a total membership of 718.

The masterly effort of Professor Prescott will be found below, also his evening talk, and the proceedings of the conference in reference to the establishment of a school.

THE SERMON BY PROFESSOR W. W. PRESCOTT.

"IN BEGINNING, PROFESSOR PRESCOTT SAID that when people met together for worship it was necessary that a solemnity and quietness should pervade an audience to be acceptable to God. He selected Deuteronomy 30:15, for the text, and said that few took a right view of life, as it was the effort of Satan to delude us in regard to it. He wished we could think of such things as realities. We have not followed cunningly devised fables, and he wished a clear conception could come before us of God the Father, the Son, the holy angels, the evil angels, as facts, not as things away off from us, but as present realities, because the Devil's efforts have been to get men to do contrary to God's command, and so he puts God in the wrong light and gives a wrong view of life and its duties. He will, if possible, shut out from our minds what God requires of us and what He is willing to do for us. I would that you could see all this in the true light, for it is because of Satan's work that we cannot see these matters truly. Here is the great controversy going on year after year—God's plans and also Satan's. God and His angels and His power against Satan and his evil ones, and sin, and we are the subject of this controversy—one striving to save, the other drawing away; the last coming to us unasked and without effort. The help of God, of Christ and good angels are freely offered to us, but we are not forced to accept—to obtain them we must ask for them. If we do not we will be drawn away. God wants to make us sons and daughters of His, He wants to purify, elevate us, to lift us up out of the miry clay and put our feet upon the rock, and put a new song in our mouth. But what does the devil want to do for us? To drag us down; to bring evil upon us; to bring sickness upon us; and to bring us down to his level. Now that is the choice. It is only because God guards us every moment that we live at all. If the devil had his way we could not assemble to learn of God. He tries ever to deceive and make the world attractive and the kingdom of the future away off, and nothing worth striving for.

"Sometimes we think the kingdom near to us, at others it loses its brightness and this world seems more desirable. What is this? Why, it is the work of the devil. He wants to make every one of us like himself. Did he ever lead you into good? He will make everything in this world so attractive that we will weigh eternal life against worldly gain. Now the greatest effort of his is to make the people believe there is no devil so that he can work unsuspected. Let us weigh these things carefully. If the thought comes to us not to be earnest in our service to God—that points from the devil. If we feel in our hearts the love due God, that is a heavenly influence. Now this conflict goes on continuously, and there are only two classes–the servants of God and the servants of the devil. This is all real. Now you can choose to be a son of God and have eternal life, or you can be a servant of Satan and be lost eternally. That is the choice set before all of us.

"Now none sit down and deliberately decide to be a servant of Satan, but we put off the decision from day to day and it apparently hangs, but is it undecided? No, just as long as we do not decide to be followers of Christ we are the servants and slaves of Satan. There is no question in that 'while they promise you liberty, they themselves are servants of corruption.' God promises us certain things but we don't make them real, do not half believe them. I hope we think we do, but if we did believe, there would not be a hesitating, doubting Christian among us. He says He will reach out His right hand and help us, but do we believe Him? This promise is not far off–his very promises, if believed, make it impossible to be doubting and hesitating. The promises are conditional. If we repent, how far? Why far enough to be sorry for our sins, and to stop sinning. He wants us to believe. How much? Why, to believe that Christ is our Saviour, and that God loved us enough (not the patriarchs alone, but us—you and I), to do this. If we believe this, it teaches us nearly, does not seem away off.

"If the cross was to be erected here, and Christ should come in and say: 'Look at the marks of the nails. This was for you.' Would it not seem real to us? Well, just so truly was it done for us. But Satan tries to force us to give our whole effort to the concerns of the things present and let the future go. It is God's desire that we shall show our appreciation, willingness and anxiety for eternal life. It is no honor to God for us to serve Him. The value of it comes from our being able to choose. No power exists that can keep us out of God's kingdom except our own will. There is no power in Heaven or earth that can save us if we will against it. It is this choice that makes living a solemn thing. There is a peculiar feeling prevalent that when we embrace Christ we drop down in the moral scale, that the worldly one is above us, but this is false. He who follows Christ is lifted up; it is only our own base views that make it seem otherwise.

"Now if the religion of Jesus Christ is worth anything, it is worth something in daily life. It ought to help us, for instance, to keep our temper. There ought not to be such a thing as a fretful Christian. There is a peace that comes into the Christian life that ought to come into our homes. When we talk of common things we live right in that place, but when we talk of Christ and His love we are lifted up into His atmosphere. There are indexes, and one can tell by the conversation how high a Christian has advanced. We certainly will talk about it. Here Satan works to keep us silent, a kind of constraint to draw us away from religious subjects. If we are really pilgrims and strangers, what will we talk about most? If we were left a legacy provided we could establish our identity, what would we do? Talk about the prospect before us would we not? Well, there is an inheritance before us. If ye are Christ's, then are ye Abraham's seed and heirs accordingly to the promise. Then have we proved up our title? Have we told our brethren about our prospects?

"These things, brethren, are realities. These are not shadows we can not grasp. There is reality in the promises of God to those who remain faithful. If we are really Christ's it will show itself not only in our home but in our relation to our neighbors. Carry our religion into our homes among our neighbors and into our business. When we come to the hard places in life who then is our helper? 'Be not dismayed for I am thy God, I will strengthen thee, yea I will help thee.' We want to be in a position where we can claim these promises. We are not isolated, we have an influence over others, and we have a responsibility in seeing that our influence is always exerted for God and His truth. There is too much shifting of responsibility to someone else, we lose sight of our own individuality. Our influence for God should be active. If no pretense of religion is made, the responsibility is the same. You can not escape this and you must answer for it. God surrounds us with circumstances and opportunities and we will have to account for them.

This is why life here is given us to prepare for the future, and in the judgment when we stand before Him stripped of everything connected with this world, the question will be, not of money, not of influence, or standing among men but of character–anything short of this is failure. God knows every one of His children and He can not be deceived. 'I know thy works.' That is encouraging to the Christian, but it is just as true of the others. 'I know thy works' is said to the sinner also. God calls upon us to be honest with ourselves and with Him. We can not deceive Him. Any pretense will be a failure. It becomes us to think seriously about these things and seek that help that will enable us to see them in a true light. God is patient and merciful and calls us to him, notwithstanding our unfaithfulness. Think how year in and year out we have turned away from God yet how patiently He has waited and how when we turn to Him, He meets us when we are a long way off. Should we not be thankful? Well then, when His spirit prompts us to come to Him and gain eternal life, we ought to be thankful to Him and listen to Him, and then if we decide to follow Christ, how careful we ought to be to walk worthy of the vocation wherewith we have been called. 'See I have set before thee this day life and good, and death and evil.'"

The evening session was devoted to the school interests, and Professor Prescott was the speaker. He said he wanted to present some practical matters.

"In view of our work as a people, it is often asked 'How long a time should be devoted by our young people to attendance at out public schools?' No general answer can be given. It will depend much upon the ages and previous opportunities. They must have time to obtain judgment and Christian experience. It is to be regretted if they are crowded out sooner than this. I have, as a rule, advised a stay of at least two years. The feeling prevails that all that is necessary to receive education sufficient to labor in the cause, and this is right, but the trouble is that we have our ideas way down. Do you think that it takes less preparation to present the truths of God than it does to labor in the same line of work in our public schools and similar positions? It requires a broader conception of what is required to have a right view of the subject. It requires more than a novice. It requires training and education, and then comes in the necessity for the help of God—the education and training being that our people may labor more successfully for God. If we had taken broader views of our needs ten years ago, we would not now be so crippled for competent helpers. 'None can be too highly educated to become humble disciples of Christ.' If you have young people capable of a high education fit them up for it. If religious training goes hand in hand with education, it is safe to give a high one. We need more cultivation, refinement and education in our laborers. It is a very nice thing to combine elevation and humility, for they belong together. Education, culture, refinement and humility ought to go together in our work. Some think that education will elevate one and lift him above common education. Such education should be despised. It is not true education. It is a glory, an outside show. The education we want is that which makes a young man or woman love still more the old father, mother, home. True education does this, makes us love each other, and God and His work, more and more. This kind of training ought to come into our own homes. If we are to dwell with God and He is to be our God, and we ought to be preparing to dwell with Him. Young people who are able to do so, give them a thorough training.

"Now another point. Why is it so necessary to go to such expense? Could we not rent a few rooms? Yes, and I suppose the school would be cheap all through. We have not only to educate, but to teach religion also, to develop these young people mentally and morally. To do this we have to provide home influences. Our homes cost more than our schools. I would rather give up the school room than the home. Now shall you move to where the school is or board your children with some family, or board them at the school? It depends upon what you are and what the family is but if the school home is what it ought to be that is the best place for your child, and if it is not what it ought to be it had better be given up. As I have watched the mental and moral growth of our young people from year to year I feel that its value can not be estimated from a money basis."

A motion was then made and carried to take the school resolution from the table and acted upon. The resolution was then read. In reply to questions in reference to the location of the school it was stated that the present resolution contemplated a school location in the Southwest, but if but one school was decided upon west of the Mississippi it would accommodate the nine conferences between that river and the Rocky Mountains. Parsons, Landis and others spoke briefly, the balance of sentiment seeming to be in favor of a school in Kansas. Mr. L.J. Rousseau said he did not think the question ought to turn out whether the school will be in Kansas or elsewhere. We ought to feel for others as well as ourselves and should try to do the best for all the children. In reply to a question it was stated that ten acres ought to be the least amount of land for a home school.

It was moved to amend the amendment so as to include all the conferences west of the Mississippi and east of the Rocky Mountains, in one school centrally located. After much discussion a motion to adjourn was made and the conference adjourned to meet on call of the chair.

The Closing Scene

CAMPMEETING GROUND, OTTAWA, Kan. May 27.

The closing scene here was the ordinance of baptism, in which thirty–three candidates took part. Elder W.W. Stebbins officiated. The bridge and banks of the stream were crowded with spectators. In every respect this has been the most successful and most largely attended of any meeting of this denomination in the state.

We invite you to view the complete
selection of titles we publish at:

www.TEACHServices.com

TEACH Services, Inc.
P U B L I S H I N G
www.TEACHServices.com ● (800) 367-1844

Scan with your mobile
device to go directly
to our website.

Please write or email us your praises, reactions,
or thoughts about this or any other book we publish at:

P.O. Box 954
Ringgold, GA 30736

info@TEACHServices.com

TEACH Services, Inc., titles may be purchased in bulk for
educational, business, fund-raising, or sales promotional use.
For information, please e-mail:

BulkSales@TEACHServices.com

Finally, if you are interested in seeing
your own book in print, please contact us at

publishing@TEACHServices.com

We would be happy to review your manuscript for free.

www.ingramcontent.com/pod-product-compliance
Lightning Source LLC
Chambersburg PA
CBHW070813100426
42742CB00012B/2347